SHEPHERD'S NOTES

SHEPHERD'S NOTES

When you need a guide through the Scriptures

John

BROADMAN
&HOLMAN
PUBLISHERS

Nashville, Tennessee

© 1998
by Broadman & Holman Publishers
Nashville, Tennessee
All rights reserved
Printed in the United States of America

1–55819–693–5
Dewey Decimal Classification: 226.50
Subject Heading: BIBLE. N.T. JOHN
Library of Congress Card Catalog Number: 97–45160

Library of Congress Cataloging-in-Publication Data
John / Dana Gould, editor
        p.   cm. — (Shepherd's notes)
    Includes bibliographical references.
    ISBN 1–55819–693–5
    1. Bible. N.T. John—Study and teaching. I. Gould, Dana, 1951–.   II. Series.
  BS2615.5.J65   1998
  226.5'07—dc21

                                                                    97–45160
                                                                         CIP

1 2 3 4 5 6   03 02 01 00 99 98

CONTENTS

FOREWORD

Dear Reader:

Shepherd's Notes are designed to give you a quick, step-by-step overview of every book of the Bible. They are not meant to be substitutes for the biblical text; rather, they are study guides intended to help you explore the wisdom of Scripture in personal or group study and to apply that wisdom successfully in your own life.

Shepherd's Notes guide you through the main themes of each book of the Bible and illuminate fascinating details through appropriate commentary and reference notes. Historical and cultural background information brings the Bible into sharper focus.

Six different icons, used throughout the series, call your attention to historical-cultural information, Old Testament and New Testament references, word pictures, unit summaries, and personal application for everyday life.

Whether you are a novice or a veteran at Bible study, I believe you will find *Shepherd's Notes* a resource that will take you to a new level in your mining and applying the riches of Scripture.

In Him,

David R. Shepherd
Editor-in-Chief

DESIGNED FOR THE BUSY USER

Shepherd's Notes for the Gospel of John is designed to provide an easy-to-use tool for getting a quick handle on this Bible book's important features, and for gaining an understanding of its message. Information available in more difficult-to-use reference works has been incorporated into the *Shepherd's Notes* format. This brings you the benefits of many more advanced and expensive works packed into one small volume.

Shepherd's Notes are for laymen, pastors, teachers, small-group leaders, and participants, as well as the classroom student. Enrich your personal study or quiet time. Shorten your class or small-group preparation time as you gain valuable insights into the truths of God's Word that you can pass along to your students or group members.

DESIGNED FOR QUICK ACCESS

Bible students with time constraints will especially appreciate the timesaving features built into *Shepherd's Notes*. All features are intended to promote a quick and concise encounter with the heart of the Bible's message.

Concise Commentary. John's narrative is replete with characters, places, events, and instruction to believers. Short sections provide quick "snapshots" of sections, highlighting important points and other information.

Outlined Text. A comprehensive outline covers the entire text of John. This is a valuable feature for following the narrative's flow, allowing for a quick, easy way to locate a particular passage.

Shepherd's Notes. Summary statements appear at the close of every key section of the narrative. While functioning in part as a quick summary, they also deliver the essence of the message presented in that section.

Icons. Various icons in the margin highlight recurring themes in John and aid in selective searching or tracing of those themes.

Sidebars and Charts. Specially selected features provide additional background information for your study or preparation. These include definitions as well as cultural, historical, and biblical information.

Maps. These are placed at appropriate places in the book to aid your understanding and study of a text or passage.

Questions to Guide Your Study. Thought-provoking questions and discussion starters are designed to encourage interaction with the truth and principles of God's Word.

In addition to the above features, study aids have been included at the back of the book for those readers who require or desire more information and resources for working through John's narrative. These include:

- chapter outlines for studying John;
- a list of reference sources used for this volume, which offer many works that allow the reader to extend the scope of his or her study of John.

DESIGNED TO WORK FOR YOU

Personal Study. Using *Shepherd's Notes* with a passage of Scripture can enrich your personal study of the Bible. At your fingertips is information that would require searching several volumes to find. In addition, many points of application occur throughout the volume, which can contribute to your biblical understanding.

Teaching. Outlines frame the text of John and provide a logical presentation of the message. *Shepherd's Notes* provide summary statements for presenting the essence of key points and events. Personal Application icons point out personal application of the message in John's Gospel, and Historical Context icons indicate where background information is supplied.

Group Study. Shepherd's Notes can be an excellent companion volume to use for gaining a quick but accurate understanding of the message of a Bible book. Each group member will benefit by having his or her own copy. The *Notes* format accommodates the study of or the tracing of themes throughout John. Leaders may use its flexible features to prepare for group sessions or use them during group sessions. Questions to Guide Your Study can spark discussion of the key points and truths of John's Gospel.

LIST OF MARGIN ICONS USED IN JOHN

Shepherd's Notes. Placed at the end of each section, a capsule statement provides the reader with the essence of the message of that section.

Old Testament Reference. To indicate a prophecy fulfillment and its discussion in the text.

New Testament Reference. Used when the writer refers to New Testament passages that are related to or have a bearing on the passage's understanding or interpretation.

Historical Background. To indicate historical, cultural, geographical, or biographical information that sheds light on the understanding or interpretation of a passage.

Personal Application. Used when the text provides a personal or universal application of truth.

Word Picture. Indicates that the meaning of a specific word or phrase is illustrated so as to shed light on it.

The Gospel of John is perhaps the most intriguing of the four accounts of the life and teaching of Jesus. In recording more than a theological treatise, John put the challenge of the Incarnation before his readers—God in human flesh.

GOSPEL OF JOHN IN A "NUTSHELL"

Purpose:	"These are written that you may believe that Jesus is the Christ, the Son of God, and that by believing you may have life in his name" (John 20:31).
Major Doctrine:	Salvation
Key Passages:	John 1:14; 3:16–21
Other Key Doctrines:	The Person and Work of Christ The Holy Spirit

AUTHOR

The authorship of the Gospel of John has been traditionally ascribed to the apostle John, the son of Zebedee and the brother of James. The Gospel itself, however, does not name its author. This has made authorship a much debated issue among interpreters. The only reference to the author is the "disciple whom Jesus loved" (21:20, 24).

The apostle John is usually seen as the author because the Gospel exhibits many marks that suggest it was written by one who was an eyewitness to the life and ministry of Jesus.

PURPOSE FOR WRITING

John included a more precise statement of purpose in his Gospel than did the other Gospel writers. From his statement in 20:31, we can see:

1. *He was selective.* His Gospel suggests that much more could have been written regarding Jesus, but only selected events are recorded.

2. *His Gospel is evangelistic.* John wanted others to believe in Jesus Christ and receive eternal life.

3. *His gospel focuses strongly on the identity of Jesus.* Jesus is not only Israel's Messiah; He is the Word of God—the Son of God.

DATE OF WRITING

Most interpreters have concluded that John's was the last of the four Gospels to be written, most likely between A.D. 60 and 90.

AUDIENCE

It is not completely clear who John's audience was. Some believe he wrote his Gospel to Jewish Christians. Others find it addressed to Jews of the dispersion.

The Jews of the dispersion were Jews scattered in various parts of the world. The diaspora took place over several centuries beginning in the eighth century before Christ. By the time John was written, as many Jews lived outside of Palestine as within it.

John's Gospel could have addressed early Christians as they worshiped and witnessed. Still, others think that it was addressed to no one in particular but to the world at large.

Therefore, looking at all three possible target audiences—Jewish, Gentile, and Christian—and all three time frames—past, present, and future—the Gospel of John was sent out into the world to convince people that Jesus Christ was God's Son, the Savior, and to challenge them to faith in Him.

LITERARY FORM

The literary form of John's Gospel is just that—a gospel.

John made use of many features of Hebrew poetry. His Gospel does not contain parables of the kind included in Matthew, Mark, and Luke but rather brings forth the many allegories Jesus used in His teaching.

KEY FEATURES IN JOHN'S GOSPEL

An emphasis on signs. In John's Gospel, a miracle is a sign. These supernatural events point to Jesus' divine origin and are witness to His deity.

An emphasis on Jesus' attendance at feasts. Within his Gospel John mentioned three Passovers, the Feast of Tabernacles, and the Feast of Dedication.

An emphasis on Jesus' Judean ministry. John's Gospel provides us with the fullest account of Jesus' ministry in Judea. John's narrative supplements the information we find in the Synoptic Gospels regarding Jesus' ministry in Judea.

Many lengthy discourses. These discourses are replete with key questions, profound answers, and dialogue. It is likely that John paraphrased Jesus' words and summarized the discourses in his own words.

THEOLOGICAL SIGNIFICANCE OF JOHN'S GOSPEL

From this Gospel we learn much about God as Father. Contemporary believers are indebted to John for their habit of referring to God simply as "the Father."

Throughout, the Gospel of John focuses on Jesus Christ. It is clear that God in Christ has revealed Himself (1:1–18). God is active in

Gospel

The word *gospel* comes from the Anglo-Saxon word *godspell*, which literally means "good news." It is a narrative of the good news of Jesus Christ. Within the New Testament, the word *euanggelion*—which is translated "gospel"—always refers to oral communication, never to a document or piece of literature. Not until the beginning of the second century and the writings of the church fathers do references to gospels—written documents—occur.

Matthew, Mark, and Luke are called the Synoptic Gospels because their view of Jesus is similar. They share much of the same content, order, and wording while having marked differences.

Christ, the Savior of the world, bringing about the salvation He has planned (4:42).

John's Gospel tells us more about the Holy Spirit than the other Gospels. The Spirit is active at the start of Jesus' ministry (1:32), but the Spirit's full work was to begin at the consummation of Jesus' own ministry (7:37–39). The Spirit brings life (3:1–8), a life of the highest quality (10:10), and leads believers in the way of truth (16:13). In this way, the Spirit multiplies Jesus' ministry for and through Christians of all ages.

ETHICAL SIGNIFICANCE OF JOHN'S GOSPEL

In response to the work of God in their lives, Christians are to be characterized by love (13:34–35). They owe all they have to the love of God, and it is proper that they respond to that love by loving God and other people.

BASIC OUTLINE OF JOHN

I. Introduction (1:1–2:11)

II. Jesus' Public Ministry (2:12–4:54)

III. Opposition to Christ (5:1–12:50)

IV. Final Words and Deeds of Christ (13:1–21:25)

QUESTIONS TO GUIDE YOUR STUDY

1. What did John want to accomplish with his Gospel?

2. Matthew, Mark, and Luke are known as the Synoptic Gospels. Why is John's Gospel different from these three Gospels?

3. What are the key themes of John's Gospel?

4. Based on this introduction, what are we to gain from a study of John's Gospel?

Jesus' Discourses in John

REFERENCE	WHERE DELIVERED	STYLE	TO WHOM	LESSON
3:1–21	Jerusalem	Conversation	Nicodemus	We must be "born of water and the Spirit" to enter the kingdom of God
4:1–30	At Jacob's Well	Conversation	Samaritan Woman	"God the Spirit" to be worshiped in spirit and truth
4:31–38	At Jacob's Well	Conversation	The Disciples	Our food is to do His will
5:1–47	Bethesda—a Pool	Conversation	The Jews	To hear Him and believe on Him is to have everlasting life
6:22–71	Capernaum	Sermon	The Multitude	Christ as the Bread of Life
7:11–40	Temple—Jerusalem	Instruction	The Jews	Judge not according to outward appearance
8:12–59	Temple—Jerusalem	Instruction	The Jews	To follow Christ is to walk in light
10:1–21	Jerusalem	Instruction	The Jews	Christ is the door; He knows His sheep; He gives His life for them

Jesus' Discourses in John

REFERENCE	WHERE DELIVERED	STYLE	TO WHOM	LESSON
12:20–50	Jerusalem	Exhortation	The People	Death for life; way of eternal life
13:1–20	Jerusalem	Exhortation	The Disciples	The lesson of humility and service
14–16	Jerusalem	Exhortation	The Disciples	The proof of discipleship: that He will come again

Miracles of Jesus in the Gospel of John

MIRACLE	PASSAGE
Water turned to wine	2:1
Healing of a royal official's son	4:46
Healing of a lame man at Bethesda	5:1
Feeding of five thousand	6:1
Walking on the sea	6:16
Healing of the blind man	9:1
Raising of Lazarus	11:38
A miraculous catch of fish	21:1

The Seven Signs in John

SIGN	REFERENCE	CENTRAL TRUTH
1. Changing water to wine	2:1–11	Points to Jesus as the source of all the blessings of God's future (see Isa. 25:6–8; Jer. 31:11–12; Amos 9:13–14)
2. Healing the official's son	4:43–54	Points to Jesus as the giver of life
3. Healing the invalid at Bethesda	5:1–15	Points to Jesus as the Father's coworker
4. Feeding the five thousand	6:1–15, 25–69	Points to Jesus as the life-giving Bread from heaven
5. Walking on water	6:16–21	Points to Jesus as the divine I AM
6. Healing the man born blind	9:1–41	Points to Jesus as the giver of spiritual sight
7. Raising Lazarus	11:1–44	Points to Jesus as the Resurrection and the Life

Pictures of Jesus in the Gospel of John

PICTURE	LESSON TAUGHT	REFERENCE
The good shepherd	Christ the only way to God	10:1–26
The vine and the branches	The need to abide in Christ	15:1–6

"I AM" Sayings in the Gospel of John

SAYING	REFERENCE
"I am the bread of life"	6:35
"I am the light of the world"	8:12
"I am the gate for the sheep"	10:7
"I am the good shepherd"	10:11, 14
"I am the resurrection and the life"	11:25
"I am the way, the truth, and the life"	14:6
"I am the true vine"	15:1, 5
"I am a king"	18:37

Titles for Jesus in John

TITLE	SIGNIFICANCE	REFERENCE
Bread of Life	The one essential food	6:35
Good Shepherd	Gives guidance and protection	10:11
Lamb of God	Offered His life as a sacrifice for sins	1:29
Light of the World	One who brings hope and gives guidance	9:5
Rabbi/Teacher	A title of respect for one who taught the Scriptures	3:2
Son of God	A title of deity signifying Jesus' unique and special intimacy with the Father	20:31
Word	Eternal God who supremely reveals God	1:1

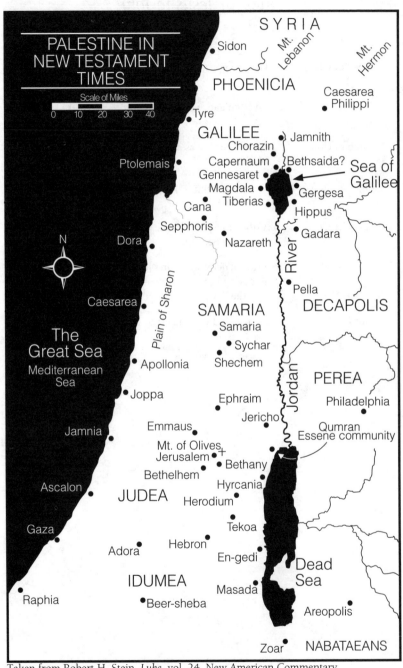

PALESTINE IN
NEW TESTAMENT
TIMES

Scale of Miles

0   10   20   30   40

SYRIA

Sidon

Mt. Lebanon

Mt. Hermon

PHOENICIA

Caesarea
Philippi

Tyre

GALILEE

Jamnith

Chorazin

Capernaum   Bethsaida?   Sea of
Gennesaret   Galilee
Magdala
Tiberias   Gergesa

Ptolemais

Hippus

Cana
Sepphoris

Nazareth

Gadara

Dora

River

Pella

DECAPOLIS

Caesarea

SAMARIA

Samaria

Plain of Sharon

Sychar
Shechem

The
Great Sea

Mediterranean
Sea

Apollonia

Joppa

Ephraim

Jericho

Jordan

PEREA

Philadelphia

Jamnia

Emmaus

Mt. of Olives
Jerusalem
Bethany

Bethelhem

Hyrcania

Qumran
Essene community

Ascalon

JUDEA

Herodium

Gaza

Tekoa

Adora

Hebron

En-gedi

Raphia

IDUMEA

Beer-sheba

Masada

Dead
Sea

Areopolis

Zoar   NABATAEANS

Taken from Robert H. Stein, *Luke*, vol. 24, New American Commentary
(Nashville, Tenn.: Broadman & Holman Publishers, 1994), p. 61.

John the Apostle

John opens his Gospel with an eloquent prologue: "In the beginning was the Word." The first eighteen verses introduce themes which John elaborates on in the rest of his Gospel.

THE PROLOGUE (1:1–18)

Meaning of the Term Word to John's First Readers

AUDIENCE	MEANING
1. Jews	Power—the Word of God that "spoke" the world into being
2. Greeks	Principle—the rational principle or rational mind that rules the universe
3. Christians	Proclamation—the preaching of the Gospel

John was the son of Zebedee and the brother of James. John is always mentioned in the first four lists of the twelve apostles. He is also among the "inner three" who were with Jesus on special occasions. Five books of the New Testament are attributed to John: this Gospel, three epistles (1, 2, 3 John), and Revelation. In each case, the traditional view that the apostle was the author of this Gospel can be traced to the following second-century writers: Irenaeus, Clement of Alexandria, and Tertullian. Neither the Gospel nor the epistles identify their author by name.

"The Word was God" (vv. 1–3)

No other book in the Bible has a prologue as overtly theological as does the Gospel of John. First, John makes a clear and decisive statement regarding the nature of Jesus: "The Word was God." John wanted it known that Jesus Christ is fully God in human form.

Word

The term *logos* was probably chosen for several reasons: because of (1) its meaning in the Old Testament, (2) its use in Greek, and (3) its use in contemporary Hebrew literature, where the concepts of *wisdom* and *word* were being spoken of as essential attributes of God. John saw that the same agent of God who created the universe was at work in a new creation inaugurated by Jesus' coming. The creative Word of God became flesh—showing forth the glory of God (John 1:14).

"The *Logos* here is more than reason, more than word; it is more than wisdom personified. The term designates a Person, distinct from and yet co-eternal and identical in essence with God—'all that God is the Logos is'" (G. Turner and Jesus Mantey, *The Gospel According to John*, p. 54).

Three Basic Affirmations of Christian Doctrine in John 1:1

AFFIRMATION	SIGNIFICANCE
1. "In the beginning was the Word"	The Word existed *before* creation
2. "The Word was with God"	The personal relationship of the Word to God
3. "The Word was God"	The Word is true deity

And yet, John makes clear that while he equates the Word with God the Word is distinct from the Father.

The Purpose of the Word (vv. 4–5)

Christ, the Word, brings life, a life that serves as the "light" for all people. The life that Christ offers is not temporal; it is eternal. It is of God. The questions and concerns of this world that find no ultimate answers are met by the Light that pierces all darkness with the brilliance of truth, yet this truth has been rejected.

John expresses two purposes with the concepts of *light* and *life*: (1) Jesus Christ came into the world to reveal the person and character of God; and (2) Christ came to redeem people.

■ *The Word that existed prior to creation has*
■ *now become human in a person, Jesus Christ*
■ *of Nazareth. The Word is now dwelling*
■ *among mankind, displaying the glory of*
■ *God and shining the Light of life in a dark,*
■ *sinful world.*

Points of Contrast Between Light and Darkness in John's Writings

LIGHT	DARKNESS
God	Satan
Truth	Lies
Holiness	Sin
Life	Death

Light

The concept of "light" appears numerous times in both the Old and New Testaments. Light was the first creation of God (Gen. 1:3). It is the source of life and energy in the universe. Light enables us to see. As with physical light, so with God. He is light—not physical light but the source of all creation. It is only in Him that we see spiritually.

THE WORLD AND THE WORD (1:6–18)

Jesus as the Light. The Word has come into the world as a Person. The witness to that Person will be given by another person. That witness is a man sent by God—John the Baptist. His purpose is to lead people to believe in the Light, who is Jesus (1:35–37). Jesus' Light is a witness to all people. Those who respond to His witness will become children of God by divine creation (1:12–13).

The Word becomes flesh. In verse 14 we have one of the most profound statements in all history. The Word who created everything became a human being—lived in a particular place and time in history. This Word dwelled among us.

Dwell

The word *dwell* means "to pitch one's tent or tabernacle.... In Revelation it is used of God tabernacling with men and here of the Logos tabernacling, God's Shekinah glory here among us in the person of his Son" (A. T. Robertson, *Word Pictures in the New Testament*, "The Fourth Gospel," vol. 5, 13).

- *In one of the most profound statements in all*
- *history, the Word took the form of a person*
- *and entered the human race. The Word has*
- *now pitched His tent among people.*

JOHN THE BAPTIST'S ROLE (1:19–28)

John's narrative now shifts from poetry to prose. He explains the relationship between John the

Baptist and Jesus Christ. John the Baptist was sent from God (1:6), but John was not himself the light (v. 8). He came as a witness to Christ (vv. 7, 15).

■ ■ *John the Baptist offered the words*
■ *of the prophet Isaiah about the*
■ *nature of his identity: "A voice of*
■ *one calling: In the desert prepare the way for*
■ *the Lord, 'Make straight the way for the*
■ *Lord'" (1:23; see Isa. 40:3). John denied*
■ *being either Isaiah or Elijah, as some pro-*
■ *posed. What was at hand in Jesus' mind was*
■ *how John became a fulfillment of the proph-*
■ *ecy recorded in Malachi 4:5.*

In this Gospel we see a threefold purpose for John's testimony:

1. To fulfill the prophecy of Isaiah 40:3.
2. To call people to repentance.
3. To draw people's attention toward the coming of the Messiah, Jesus Christ.

■ *John the Baptist had a distinct role as fore-*
■ *runner to the Messiah's coming. His purpose,*
■ *rooted in a prophecy of Isaiah, was to call*
■ *people to repentance and point them to the*
■ *coming Messiah.*

THE LAMB OF GOD (1:29–34)

John the Baptist's confession upon seeing Jesus—that here was "the Lamb of God, who takes away the sin of the world" (v. 29)—was of great significance.

The Jews used a lamb as a sacrifice for the Passover Feast, which celebrated Israel's deliverance from bondage in Egypt. Isaiah offered the idea of the Suffering Servant in terms of a sacrificial lamb (Isa. 53). John is declaring that Jesus is the true sacrificial lamb for the Passover; His death would now serve as the deliverance of God's people from their sins. As Paul wrote in his letter to the church at Corinth, "Christ, our Passover lamb, has been sacrificed" (1 Cor. 5:7).

John the Baptist then gave testimony that he saw "the Spirit come down and remain" on Jesus (v. 32). This confirmed to John that Jesus was the Messiah. Then he declared: "I have seen and I testify that this is the Son of God" (v. 34).

- *Jesus is the true sacrificial lamb; His death*
- *would serve as the deliverance of God's peo-*
- *ple from their sins.*

JESUS CALLS HIS DISCIPLES (1:35–51)

Andrew and Another Disciple (vv. 35–42)

The calling of Andrew, Simon Peter's brother, was the direct result of John the Baptist's testimony about Jesus as the Lamb of God. John did not name the second disciple mentioned in the narrative, but some believe it was the apostle John himself.

After spending an evening with Jesus, Andrew found his brother and made a startling announcement: "We have found the Messiah" (v. 41). He then brought Simon to Jesus.

Upon encountering Simon, Jesus gave him a new nickname, Cephas.

Philip and Nathaniel (vv. 43–51)

Jesus took the initiative in calling Philip. His simple invitation was, "Follow me" (v. 43). Philip then shared his experience with Christ with another, Nathaniel. He gave testimony to Nathaniel that the One to whom the Scriptures gave witness had been found. At first, Nathaniel was skeptical, but upon meeting Jesus, he turned from his skepticism to faith.

Son of Man

The term *Son of Man* is a messianic term that has its roots in the Old Testament. It is the term Jesus used most often to identify Himself. The term went beyond classifying Jesus as a human. It also pointed to His heavenly origin and His glory. It spoke of His lowliness and humility in showing God to others through His suffering.

Cephas/Peter

The names "Cephas" (Aramaic) and "Peter" (Greek) both mean *rock*. That Peter would be given this name is interesting because he was anything but "rocklike." Peter was impulsive and undisciplined in spirit, a rough-hewn man of raw emotion. Yet Christ called those whom He would develop, and Peter would indeed become the pillar of the church, the "rock" upon which the early church would depend (Matt. 19:16; Acts 2).

■ *Jesus began to choose His disciples. Included*
■ *in this first group of four was Simon, to*
■ *whom Jesus gave a new name—Cephas,*
■ *meaning "rock."*

QUESTIONS TO GUIDE YOUR STUDY

1. What meaning was John trying to convey to his readers with the term *Word*?
2. What is the significance of the Word becoming flesh?
3. What was John the Baptist's role in relation to the Messiah?
4. What themes did John introduce in this first chapter?

This chapter begins a major division of John's Gospel that deals with the signs Jesus used to point beyond Himself to a truth about God. The eleven chapters of this section have to do with Jesus' public ministry.

TURNING WATER INTO WINE (2:1–11)

Sign

The Gospel of John uses the word *sign* rather than *miracle*. Signs served as authentication for Jesus' nature and mission. Further, a sign points beyond itself to a major truth about God made known through Jesus Christ. Throughout the section of John's Gospel that deals with Jesus' signs, a miracle is always a sign that points beyond the event of the miracle to a greater truth.

The First Sign: Changing Water to Wine

SIGN	CHARACTER-ISTIC OF JESUS' POWER	RESULT OR RESPONSE TO THE SIGN
Jesus causes water to change into wine.	Creative	The disciples believed in Jesus.

The Sign (vv. 1–10)

Jesus' first miracle was at a wedding at Cana of Galilee.

During the wedding festivities, the wine ran out unexpectedly. Not only was this an embarrassing situation for the wedding family, but it could also expose them to legal liability. Mary informed Jesus that the wine supply had been exhausted. At the proper time, Jesus instructed servants to fill several stone waterpots with water. He then had them draw out some water and take it to the steward of the feast. The

Cana was about eight miles north of Jesus' hometown, Nazareth.

steward, upon tasting the wine, remarked that the quality of the wine was better than before.

The Meaning of the Sign (v. 11)

With Jesus there is full and complete revelation of God. He brings new joy into life. When the old life has gone flat, Jesus introduces a new joy and vitality.

Numbers often have a symbolic meaning in the Bible. Seven is the number of completion, whereas the number six indicates something just short of completion. Six waterpots were used, which are connected to Jewish ritual observances. The knowledge the Jews had of God and their relationship to Him through the Jewish law was incomplete. *One* was needed to make it complete—Jesus.

The water, used for purification, is replaced with wine, which would come to symbolize the blood of Christ. The blood of Christ did indeed supplant the Jewish ceremonial system in regard to the problem of sin and a holy God's demand for righteousness.

■ *Jesus performed His first miracle by turning*
■ *water into wine. It was symbolic. As the com-*
■ *plete revelation of God, Jesus brings new joy*
■ *into life.*

JESUS CLEARS OUT THE TEMPLE (2:12–25)

All four Gospels include the incident of Jesus' cleansing the Temple. In this act, Jesus brought forth God's standards of right and wrong.

It was Passover, the time of remembering how God had delivered Israel from bondage in Egypt. Jesus encountered individuals who were profiteering from the religious festival.

Jesus saw these merchants taking advantage of the pilgrims to Jerusalem. He was incensed by what He saw and made a whip out of cords. Jesus then overturned the tables of the money changers and chased them and their animals from the Temple. He then charged the money changers with making the house of God a house of trade.

This spectacle aroused the indignation of the Jews. Their concern was not the moral issue of whether the sellers and money changers should have been there but rather on what grounds Jesus took it upon Himself to expel them. When the Jews called for a "sign," Jesus responded, "Destroy this temple, and I will raise it again in three days" (v. 18). Jesus was referring to the temple of His body.

A result of this cleansing of the Temple was that Jesus introduced a new kind of worship. Whereas the money changers had substituted convenience for compassion and sacrifice for submission, Jesus showed that the Father demands instead sincerity and truth in worship.

Money Changing in the Temple

Money changers were present at the Temple to exchange Roman or other money for Jewish money acceptable in the Temple worship. Worshipers could also purchase birds and animals used for sacrifice. Since sacrificial birds and animals had to be officially certified and unblemished, it was helpful to purchase them at the Temple. Some exchangers profited greatly by loaning their money. Their interest rates ranged from 20 to 300 percent per year. Evidently, the selling and money changing had become a means of cheating and exploiting the people. In anger at this corruption of the purpose of the Temple, Jesus turned over the tables of the money changers and drove them and the sellers of animals out of the Temple court.

■ *Incensed at what was taking place at the*
■ *Temple, Jesus used a whip and drove the*
■ *money changers from the Temple. Although*
■ *the Jewish authorities were indignant, Jesus*
■ *succeeded in showing that the Father*
■ *demands sincerity and truth in worship.*

QUESTIONS TO GUIDE YOUR STUDY

1. John's Gospel presents seven signs, the first of which appears in this chapter. What is a sign, and what is its purpose?

2. Who were the money changers, and what were they doing in the Temple?

3. Why did Jesus clear the Temple? What resulted from this incident?
4. What did Jesus mean with His statement, "Destroy this temple, and I will raise it again in three days"?

JOHN 3

This chapter deals with the theme of the new birth and contains perhaps the most familiar verse in the Bible: John 3:16. This verse is often referred to as "the Bible in miniature."

GOD'S SAVING LOVE (3:1–21)

Nicodemus Learns of the New Birth (vv. 1–15)

Nicodemus had everything: power, prestige, and position. He was a member of the Sanhedrin, a council of seventy elders—a group that was most interested in following the Law precisely. Yet he decided to visit Jesus at night. In spite of all he had, he wanted to know more about Jesus' teaching. This conversation between Nicodemus and Jesus is the first discourse John recorded in his Gospel.

Nicodemus opened the conversation with Jesus with a compliment by calling Him "Rabbi." *Rabbi* means "teacher." Although Nicodemus knew that Jesus was not formally trained, he apparently had observed that God was a part of what Jesus had been doing.

Jesus got to the heart of the matter and His message: "No one can see the kingdom of God unless he is born again" (v. 3). A startling statement indeed to Nicodemus! He began to interpret it literally and questioned the possibility of being physically reborn. Rephrasing His statement, Jesus asserted that unless one is born of both "water and the Spirit" a person cannot enter the kingdom of God. Jesus clarified that He was speaking about a spiritual rebirth, not a physical one.

Nicodemus

His name means "conqueror of the people." John identified Nicodemus as a Pharisee and a member of the Sanhedrin, the Jewish ruling council. He was a "teacher of Israel," that is, an authority on the interpretation of the Hebrew Scriptures. The reference to Nicodemus's initial coming at night to see Jesus highlights his later public participation in Jesus' burial (John 19:39–41). His contribution was aloes and spices, enough to prepare a king for burial.

Water and the Spirit

There is some debate about the meaning of *water*. Because the Pharisees were aware of John the Baptist's baptism, Jesus could have been alluding to John's baptism for repentance. His baptism suggested repentance from the former manner of life. The meaning of *Spirit* is quite clear, as it was a reference to the spiritual rebirth—regeneration —brought about by the activity of the Holy Spirit in a human life.

Born of water could also refer to physical birth. Jesus contrasted this with being born of the Spirit. "Unless one is born of water and the Spirit, he cannot enter into the kingdom of God. That which is born of the flesh is flesh, and that which is born of the Spirit is spirit" (John 3:5–6).

The Good News of Jesus Christ (vv. 16–21)

There can be little doubt that this section of John's narrative is the most familiar in all of Scripture, with verse 16 serving as the most familiar single verse in all the Bible. There is good reason, for John 3:16 presents the clearest, simplest statement of the good news of Jesus Christ.

There are three key aspects to the good news:

1. God loves us.
2. God's love is so great that He sent His only Son to tell the world about God's love.
3. Anyone who believes in God's Son will never die but will live forever with God.

Belief means far more than intellectual assent to the claims of Christ. It means placing one's life and trust in complete surrender to the one in whom we believe. (See the article "Belief in the New Testament" at the back of this book.)

- ■ *To enter the kingdom of God, one must be*
- ■ *"born again." Because of His love for us, God*
- ■ *sent His only Son into the world to save us.*
- ■ *The good news of Jesus Christ is that by*
- ■ *believing in Him we can be born again and*
- ■ *receive eternal life.*

JESUS, THE DISCIPLER (3:22–36)

When students of the life of Christ list the priorities of His ministry, many items come to mind: the miracles, the teaching of the multitudes, the Crucifixion, and the Resurrection. But one of Jesus' top priorities was discipling twelve men. This required time, and He took the time (v. 22) to prepare these men for the time when He would no longer be visibly present.

During this time, an argument developed between some of John's disciples and the Jewish leaders over ceremonial cleansing. The appropriate means of achieving ceremonial cleansing of their bodies and eating utensils was of great interest to the Jewish community. When the matter was brought to John, the question of Jesus' ministry in relation to John's ministry surfaced. The loyalty of these disciples to their master, John, is evident as they allowed envy to enter into their thinking about Jesus. John's reply affirmed his previous testimony about Jesus. It also provided an important insight into John's character.

Knowing a teachable moment had presented itself, John informed his students that one "can receive only what is given him from heaven" (v. 27).

John knew that he was "from the earth," whereas Jesus, as God's Son, was "from heaven" (v. 31). John taught his disciples that their relation with God's Son had eternal consequence.

Those who believe in and obey Jesus have eternal life. Those who don't believe and obey are in sin and have the abiding wrath of God on them.

John the Baptist

John the Baptist was a prophet from a priestly family. He preached a message of repentance, announced the coming of the Messiah, baptized Jesus, and was beheaded by Herod Antipas. John's clothing reminded the people of the ancient prophet Elijah (cp. 2 Kings 1:8). It was generally believed that Elijah would return just before the Messiah made His appearance. John wore camel's hair clothing with a leather girdle. His diet would be considered repulsive by most Westerners. He lived off the land, eating insects (such as locusts, an excellent source of protein) and wild honey (Matt. 3:4).

- *This section is a clarification of the question*
- *of the followers of John the Baptist. It also*
- *answers the controversy that might arise*
- *between the followers of John and the church.*
- *Jesus is the new Master. John had simply*
- *pointed the way.*

Wrath

The Greek word for *wrath* is *orge*, which denotes God's abiding opposition to sin.

23

The point of this affirmation is clear. Knowing God has given everything, one who loves God will not envy another person's gifts, abilities, or accomplishments. John understood his role in relation to Jesus as that of "the best man" to the groom at a wedding. John instructed those who had supported and followed his ministry that Jesus must become greater, while he, John, "must become less" (v. 30).

QUESTIONS TO GUIDE YOUR STUDY

1. What do we know about Nicodemus? Why was he interested in what Jesus had to say?

2. The "new birth" is the heart of Jesus' message. What does it means to be "born again"?

3. In referring to the new birth, what did Jesus mean when He said that those who are born again are born of "water and Spirit"?

4. What question did John's disciples ask concerning Jesus? What was John's reply?

The key event of this chapter is Jesus' encounter with the Samaritan woman. This account provides us with an excellent model for considering the nature and strategy of evangelistic outreach.

JESUS THE SOURCE OF LIFE (4:1–26)

Not wanting to be seen in competition with John's ministry, Jesus returned to Galilee. On that journey He passed through Samaria. Most Jews went out of their way to avoid Samaria. Not Jesus. Samaria was a part of His mission. The division between the Jews and Samaritans was legendary and one that Jesus refused to recognize.

Jesus' excursion into Samaria resulted in one of the most fascinating dialogues recorded in all of Scripture. Resting near a well, Jesus encountered a Samaritan woman who had been living a life of habitual immorality. Their conversation proceeded upon two levels, the spiritual and the temporal, with the woman constantly finding excuses to counter Jesus' probing of her life.

Her first shock was that Jesus would even speak to her, a Samaritan woman, considering the animosity between Jews and Samaritans. Jesus responded not to her questions but to her needs, offering her the opportunity to receive "living water" (v. 10).

Here we see much regarding the intent of Jesus' ministry, which was to bring people to a realization of the state of their life in order to lead them to repentance and a new life in Him. In their new lives they honor and worship God in spirit and truth daily. In His answer, Jesus freed worship from the limitations of place. The location

Samaritans were rejected by Jews primarily because of their mixed Gentile blood and their differing style of worship, which centered on Mount Gerizim. On this mountain the Samaritans had built a temple that rivaled the Jewish temple in Jerusalem. Samaritans insisted on worshiping at Mount Gerizim even after their temple was destroyed.

25

"Both for perplexity and for dulled conscience the remedy is the same: sincere and spiritual worship. For worship is the submission of all our nature to God. It is the quickening of conscience by His holiness; the nourishment of mind with His truth; the purifying of imagination by His beauty; the opening of the heart to His love; the surrender of will to His purpose—and all of this gathered up in adoration, the most selfless emotion of which our nature is capable and therefore the chief remedy for that self-centeredness which is our original sin that is the source of all actual sin" (J. Temple, *Readings in St. John's Gospel*, p. 68.)

of worship is not important, but the object of worship is!

■ *In His encounter with the Samaritan*
■ *woman at the well, we see much regarding*
■ *the intent of Jesus' ministry, which was to*
■ *bring people to a realization of the state of*
■ *their lives that leads them to repentance and*
■ *a new life in Him.*

THE MESSIAH'S MISSION (4:27–38)

When the disciples rejoined Jesus, they did not dare ask Him about His conversation with the Samaritan woman but rather inquired about His physical well-being. Perhaps they thought hunger had deprived Him of His senses, as He should have known better than to talk with such a woman. Jesus then continued the disciples' education, instructing them that His "food" was to "do the will of him who sent me and to finish his work" (v. 34).

■ *As Messiah, Jesus' mission was to confront*
■ *all people with the saving, liberating truth of*
■ *Himself.*

JESUS AS THE SAVIOR OF THE WORLD (4:39–42)

Jesus' encounter with the woman at the well and her subsequent sharing of that conversation resulted in many Samaritans believing in Jesus. After they met Jesus themselves, they believed not because of what the woman had said but because they had come to believe themselves "that this man really is the Savior of the world"

(v. 42). This confession of the Samaritan believers—that Jesus is the Savior—is found only here and in 1 John 4:14. Only through Jesus is the world able to be saved, and this salvation is indeed for everyone in the world.

THE HEALING OF THE OFFICIAL'S SON (4:43–54)

The Second Sign: The Healing of the Official's Son

MIRACLE PERFORMED	CHARACTERISTIC OF JESUS' POWER	RESULT OR RESPONSE TO THE SIGN
Jesus heals a boy from a great distance by His word	Master of *distance, space*	The official believed in Jesus

After His time in Samaria, Jesus returned to Galilee. There He met a royal official whose child was near death. Jesus commented how the belief of the Galileans was tied to His production of miraculous signs and wonders. This provided an interesting contrast, for the Samaritans believed "because of his words" (v. 41), while the Jews believed because of "miraculous signs and wonders" (v. 48). As Jesus would later say to Thomas following His resurrection, "Blessed are those who have not seen and yet have believed" (John 20:29).

Jesus was clearly on a mission, one that was God informed and God directed. What was that mission? To confront people—all people, as the Samaritan woman demonstrated—with the truth of Himself. Jesus told them that the fields were "ripe for harvest" (v. 35) and that in entering the field for work it made no difference whether one plants the seed or brings in the crop. This is an important truth, for there should never be competition among Christians regarding differing fields of service. All should share in the joy of seeing the kingdom of God expanded.

■ *Jesus' second sign was a miracle of healing*
■ *the official's son, who had become very ill.*
■ *This sign demonstrated His mastery over the*
■ *limitations of distance or space.*

QUESTIONS TO GUIDE YOUR STUDY

1. Why was it considered so strange for Jesus to speak to the Samaritan woman?
2. What did John mean by the phrase *living water* in describing this story?
3. What was the Messiah's mission?
4. Jesus' second sign was the healing of the official's son. What does this sign show us?

Starting with this section of John's narrative, we see an increasing reaction to Jesus' ministry. Each incident of controversy is set within the context of a Jewish festival, which serves to heighten the dramatic effect of the religious leaders' opposition to Jesus. Also, John uses the third sign to develop the theme of unbelief.

JESUS HEALS AN INVALID (5:1–5)

The Third Sign:
The Healing of the Invalid at Bethesda

MIRACLE PERFORMED	CHARACTERISTIC OF JESUS' POWER	RESULT OR RESPONSE TO THE SIGN
Jesus heals a man who has been ill for thirty-eight years	Master of *time*	The Jews begin persecuting Jesus

After an unspecified period of time, Jesus traveled to Jerusalem for a "feast of the Jews" (v. 1).

Jesus passed by the Bethesda pool, where several invalids had placed themselves. The waters, when stirred, supposedly had miraculous powers of healing. Jesus asked a man who had been there for thirty-eight years an interesting question: "Do you want to get well?" (v. 6) In Jesus' day, many people depended on their unfortunate condition for financial support given by healthy individuals out of pity.

Another possible reason for Jesus' question relates to the man's spirit. Many who have

The name of this feast is not mentioned, but it was probably one of the three pilgrimage feasts that all Jewish males were expected to attend: Passover, Pentecost, or Tabernacles.

experienced prolonged pain or misfortune have surrendered even the will to attempt to overcome their situation in life. When the invalid shared with Jesus his difficulty of getting into the pool for healing, Jesus proclaimed: "Get up! Pick up your mat and walk" (v. 8). The man was healed instantly.

This healing took place on a Sabbath. The Jewish leader's response was not joy over the man's healing but concern that he was violating the Sabbath by carrying his mat!

The Law of Moses did not forbid such a practice; only the Jewish *interpretation* of the Law of Moses forbade it. Jesus found the healed man, and as with the Samaritan woman at the well, addressed the deeper condition of the man's relationship with God. Jesus' words are interesting: "Stop sinning or something worse may happen to you" (v. 14).

- *Jesus' third sign of His power, the healing of*
- *an invalid, showed His mastery over time.*
- *With the healing, Jesus emphasized that the*
- *consequences of sin are far more serious than*
- *any form of physical illness we might have.*

THE SON OF GOD (5:16–30)

John now informs his readers that because of this healing on the Sabbath, the Jews began to persecute Jesus. This is the first recorded hostility toward Jesus in John's narrative. Jesus' view of God ran counter to that of the religious leaders.

Jesus then rebuked the leaders for their response. This rebuke outraged the Jews because "he was even calling God his own

Father, making himself equal with God" (v. 18). The Jews did not object to the idea of God as Father. They were concerned that Jesus some- how was in a special relationship to God as His Father, thus intimating that Jesus was equal with God.

Jesus then gave a clearly defined, seven-point response about the relationship between the Father (God) and the Son (Himself).

1. The Son can do nothing without the Father (vv. 19, 30).

2. The Father loves the Son and reveals everything to Him (v. 20).

3. The power to bestow life itself is shared by the Father and the Son (v. 21).

4. God has given all judgment over to the Son (v. 22).

5. The Father and the Son share equal honor (v. 23).

6. Belief in the words of the Son result in eternal life (v. 24).

7. The very consummation of the age will be by and through the Son (vv. 25–30).

The Jews objected to Jesus' answer because of their staunch monotheism (belief in one God). Christians are monotheists as well yet maintain that the nature of the one true God is that He is Triune—three persons (Father, Son, and Holy Spirit), one God.

To the Jewish mind, Jesus' claim to be God was blasphemous because it suggested the idea of two Gods. Of course, nothing of the sort was in mind with Jesus' self-declaration as the Son of God. Rather, Jesus proclaimed that He was God in human form, the second person of the Trinity.

"In gratitude of this divine gift the man was enjoined to sin no more; . . . he should not let the bitter memory of 38 tragic years continue to separate him from God. Bad as it had been to lie on a mat for most of his life, it would be even worse to be spiritually deformed, for God does not judge sickness, but he does judge sin" (Wm. Hull, *The Broadman Bible Commentary*, vol. 9, p. 263).

Legalism is a dreadful distortion of God's will for those whom He created to live in fellowship with Him. The attitudes of the heart, not just outer deeds, matter to God. When the inner world is ordered so as to give first place to God and His will, the outer world will exhibit holiness—a holiness seen in the life and ministry of Jesus.

■ *Jesus made the bold claim that He was the*
■ *Son of God. Interpreting it correctly as His*
■ *claim to be equal with God, the Jews were*
■ *incensed.*

TESTIMONY TO JESUS (5:31–47)

Throughout his narrative, John links the theme of *witness* to the theme of belief. Jesus' defense statement included five witnesses that give testimony to His claim to be the Son of man. These include John the Baptist (v. 33), the works of Jesus (v. 36), God Himself (v. 37), the Scriptures (v. 39), and Moses (v. 46).

The witness of John the Baptist (vv. 31–35)

It was John the Baptist who first declared that Jesus was "the Lamb of God, who takes away the sin of the world" (1:29).

The witness of works of Jesus (v. 36)

These were the powerful acts of Jesus done on earth in cooperation with the Father (cp. 5:20; 9:4; 10:25, 32, 37–38; 14:10–11; 15:24).

The witness of the Father (v. 37)

Three times the Father's witness came verbally during Jesus' ministry (Luke 3:22; 9:35; John 12:28–30).

The witness of the Scriptures (vv. 39–44)

The Scriptures were the foundation of His opponents, tradition. What they sought in their studies of the Scriptures could only be found in Jesus. But the leaders would not accept His witness or His claims based on the Scriptures. Included in the Old Testament Scriptures was the witness of Moses (vv. 45–47).

With these witnesses, Jesus clearly distinguished the worth of human testimony from God's testimony (vv. 34, 41, 44).

■ *Witness and belief are two key themes that*
■ *John links in his Gospel. In His defense state-*
■ *ment to the Jews, Jesus included five wit-*
■ *nesses that give testimony to His claim to be*
■ *the Son of man.*

QUESTIONS TO GUIDE YOUR STUDY

1. What was significant about Jesus' third sign?
2. Why did Jesus' healing of the invalid cause a controversy with the religious leaders?
3. The first recorded hostility toward Jesus in John's narrative has to do with Jesus' view that He is the Son of God. Why did this cause such a furor among the Jewish leaders?
4. What witnesses gave testimony to Jesus' claim to be the Son of man?

This chapter contains several of Jesus' divine acts, including two of the seven signs. It also shows this period to be a time of testing for the disciples. In these verses they faced three tests as they dealt with the needs and reactions of the crowds: (1) addressing the hunger of the five thousand; (2) dealing with Jesus' popularity with the crowd; and (3) their choice to follow the crowd or remain with Jesus.

FEEDING THE FIVE THOUSAND (6:1–15)

The Fourth Sign:
The Feeding of the Five Thousand

MIRACLE PERFORMED	CHARACTERISTIC OF JESUS' POWER	RESULT OR RESPONSE TO THE SIGN
Jesus multiplies the bread and fish to feed the crowd	Master of *quantity*	The crowd wanted to make Jesus king

The feeding of the five thousand is the one miracle, apart from the Resurrection, that occurs in all four Gospels. The number of people fed was actually far greater than five thousand, for this figure referred only to the men, since women and children were not counted (Matt. 14:21).

At a time of human hopelessness Jesus took over. He had the disciples seat the people in a grassy area. Then Jesus took bread and fish given to Him by a boy, blessed the food, and gave it to the people. There was enough to satisfy the hunger of all the people. What seemed to be a hopeless situation was turned into a scene of hope by the power of God working through Jesus.

This sign pointed to the divine nature of Jesus, demonstrated by His power and authority over the natural, created world. The crowds seemed more interested in Jesus' signs than in His truth. This miracle led the people to try to make Jesus king by force. God's design was not that Jesus manifest Himself as an earthly king but as the Suffering Servant who would give His life as a ransom for many (Mark 10:45). The result of this miracle was that some people began to believe that Jesus was indeed the prophet greater than Moses that the Scriptures had prophesied.

Not only did Jesus meet the needs of the people, but He also supplied them with more than enough. This was a lesson to the people, and to us today as well, that God through Jesus Christ provides more than is adequate for human needs.

Sea of Galilee

The place name means "circle." The sea is a freshwater lake nestled in the hills of northern Palestine. Its surface is nearly 700 feet below the level of the Mediterranean Sea, which is some thirty miles west. It is fed mainly by the Jordan River. The nearby hills of Galilee are about 1,500 feet above sea level. The lake is thirteen miles long and eight miles wide at its greatest east-west distance. Because of its location, it is subject to sudden and violent storms of short duration.

- *The fourth sign was Jesus' miracle of the*
- *feeding of the five thousand. His provision*
- *was more than sufficient. In meeting the*
- *need of the crowd, not only did Jesus show*
- *His power over the natural, created world;*
- *He also showed that He was the master of*
- *quantity.*

JESUS WALKS ON THE WATER (6:16–21)

Jesus dismissed the crowd and sent His disciples to cross the Sea of Galilee without Him. Sensing that the crowd wanted to make Him king, Jesus retreated to the hills to be alone. The crowd was more interested in a Messiah who healed the sick and fed the hungry. But Jesus' kingdom would be spiritual rather than political.

As the disciples rowed across the lake, the winds picked up and a storm arose. As the disciples

The Fifth Sign: Jesus' Walking on Water

MIRACLE PERFORMED	CHARACTERISTIC OF JESUS' POWER	RESULT OR RESPONSE TO THE SIGN
Jesus walks on the wind-whipped waves to meet the disciples' boat	Master over *natural law*	Matthew tells us that the disciples worshiped Jesus as the Son of God

approached the halfway point across (about three or four miles), they saw Jesus walking toward them on the water. Not recognizing that it was Jesus, the disciples were terrified. In another situation of human hopelessness and fear, Jesus gave hope and assurance: "It is I; don't be afraid" (v. 20). Other Gospel accounts of this event tell us that Jesus calmed the wind and waves. According to John's account, the boat immediately reached its destination at the other shore.

■ *By walking on the water, Jesus showed His*
■ *mastery over nature. Through their experi-*
■ *ences with Jesus, they learned much about*
■ *who Jesus is and about the nature of God's*
■ *kingdom.*

THE BREAD OF LIFE (6:22–59)

After the feeding of the many thousands, it is not surprising that these same people sought Jesus again. When they found Him, Jesus read their hearts and confronted them with their motive: "You are looking for me, not because you saw miraculous signs, but because you ate

"I AM" Saying: The Bread of Life (v. 35)

Statement	Significance
"I am the bread of life" (v. 35).	Jesus satisfies our deepest spiritual needs

the loaves and had your fill" (v. 26). Jesus then encouraged them not to devote themselves to such pursuits but rather to seek "food that endures to eternal life" (v. 27).

He reminded them of their forefathers during the years of wilderness wandering and how God provided them with manna to meet their physical needs: "He gave them bread from heaven to eat" (v. 31). Jesus then compared the Israelites' physical needs to the spiritual needs of His audience. "I am the bread of life. He who comes to me will never go hungry, and he who believes in me will never thirst. . . . I am the bread that came down from heaven" (vv. 35, 41). This the first of seven "I am" statements recorded in John's Gospel.

Comparison Between Manna and Jesus: The Bread of Life

Manna	Jesus
Came at night	Came when men were in darkness
Met physical need	Meets spiritual needs
A gift from God	God's gift to the world
Had to be picked up and eaten	Must be received and appropriated

I tell you the truth

This phrase, translated by the NIV as "I tell you the truth," begins with *"amen, amen"* in the Greek text. The NRSV translates this text as "truly, truly I say to you." This formula is a teaching technique that indicated a crucial idea from Jesus. It occurs in verses 26, 32, 47, and 53.

In His bread of life discourse, Jesus made several bold statements:

1. No one can come to the Father through Christ except as the Father wills (v. 44).
2. To be in a relationship with God is to be in a relationship with Jesus (v. 45).
3. Only the Son, Jesus, has seen the Father (v. 46).
4. The Bread of life is that which came down from heaven. Only by eating that bread can eternal life be gained.

■ *Jesus is the Bread of life, and only He can sat-*
■ *isfy the deep spiritual needs of people. One*
■ *may appropriate eternal life only by receiv-*
■ *ing Jesus Christ as Savior.*

THE HOLY ONE OF GOD (6:60–71)

Some Disciples Abandon Jesus (vv. 60–69)

Jesus' Bread of life discourse was not well received by all of His followers: "This is a hard teaching. Who can accept it?" (v. 60). Many followers grumbled and turned their backs on Jesus. When Jesus asked the Twelve if they also wanted to depart, they remained with their Master. Peter responded for them all: "Lord, to whom shall we go? You have the words of eternal life. We believe and know that you are the Holy One of God" (vv. 68–69).

The Holy One to Be Betrayed (vv. 70–71)

But all was not well. Jesus knew from the beginning which disciple would eventually betray Him. Jesus informed the Twelve that "one of you is a devil" (v. 70), referring to Judas.

No longer followed him

The word for *follow* is a term composed of two words in the Greek language: *alongside* and *walk*. Those disciples who abandoned Jesus were no longer willing to walk beside Him. They were no longer committed to Him and His mission. This word (*peripatein*) is used to epitomize discipleship.

■ *Recognizing Jesus to be "the Holy One of*
■ *God," the Twelve chose not to follow the*
■ *crowd but to remain with Him.*

QUESTIONS TO GUIDE YOUR STUDY

1. What does the miracle of feeding the five thousand teach us?
2. What lessons might the disciples have learned from their experience in the storm on the Sea of Galilee? What principles from this passage might we apply to the "storms" we face in our own lives?
3. What did Jesus mean when He claimed to be the Bread of Life? What does that mean to you?
4. Why was it so difficult for some disciples to continue following Jesus? What made Jesus' discourse on the Bread of life a "hard teaching" to them?

························

This chapter begins the section some call "the period of conflict." The religious leaders, having witnessed Jesus' signs and miracles and having listened to His sermons, now began to oppose Him.

GOD'S TIME (7:1–13)

Some might wonder why Jesus would stay away from Judea because the Jews there were waiting to take His life, especially in light of the fact that Jesus willingly went to death at the time of His crucifixion. Simply put, it was not His time (vv. 6–8). The time for surrendering His life would come, but not now; God desired more to be accomplished through Jesus' life. All would transpire at the moment God intended.

AN AUTHORITATIVE TEACHER (7:14–24)

At the appropriate time, halfway through the Feast of Tabernacles, Jesus revealed Himself and began to teach. The crowds were surprised that Jesus had not studied under any of the noted Jewish scholars. Jesus responded to their amazement. His teaching was not His "own," but it came "from him who sent me" (v. 16).

Jesus provided three lines of support for His teaching:

1. *His authority*. It was rooted in the Father who sent Him.
2. *His selfless ministry*. What He had done was not for self-glorification.
3. *The place of the Law*. The Jews cherished the Law of Moses but did not keep it.

The Feast of Tabernacles

The Feast of Tabernacles was observed in the fall. It consisted of celebration and thanksgiving for the fall harvest, especially the grape harvest, and commemoration of the wilderness wanderings. One of the three feasts which Jewish men were required to attend, it got its name from the use of temporary booths or tabernacles erected in the vineyards during the harvest to guard the fields. Lasting a full week—eight days with a Sabbath added at the end, it was a popular festival among the people.

■ *Jesus' authoritative teaching astonished the*
■ *festival crowd. Jesus responded by providing*
■ *authoritative support for His teaching.*

THE SPIRIT PROMISED (7:25–44)

Many people believed that no one would know the origin or birthplace of the Messiah. Therefore, since they knew of Jesus' origins, He could not be the Messiah (v. 27), according to their perspective. As a result, they tried to seize Jesus, but apparently they were unable to lay a hand on Him because "his time had not yet come" (v. 30).

One of the features of the Feast of Tabernacles was the carrying of a jar of water from the pool of Siloam to the Temple each day. Each morning a procession of priests carried the water, which was poured into a bowl at the altar while the trumpet sounded and the people shouted. Against this symbolic background, Jesus showed up at the feast on the last day.

■ *For those who believed in Him, Jesus prom-*
■ *ised to satisfy their spiritual thirst by provid-*
■ *ing "streams of living water." This "living*
■ *water" represented the Holy Spirit, who*
■ *would be poured out on believers on the day*
■ *of Pentecost.*

A PROPHET FROM GALILEE? (7:45–52)

The Temple guards sent to arrest Jesus exclaimed, "No one ever spoke the way this man does" (v. 46). The Pharisees dismissed the guards as deceived, arguing that since none of the Pharisees had expressed belief in Jesus, then

Jesus claimed that in Him might be found the fulfillment of all which this ritual represented. In addition, those who slaked their spiritual thirst at this spring would become fountains for the spiritual refreshment of others. . . . He who trusts in Christ not only receives the water of life that springs up to eternal life, but becomes the source of that gift to others. For no one can possess (or, rather, be indwelt by) the Spirit of God and keep that Spirit to himself. Where the Spirit is, He flows forth; if there is not flowing forth, He is not there.
(Wm. E. Temple's , *Readings in St. John's Gospel,* p. 130).

He was not to be accepted. The Pharisees elevated their own sense of learning and understanding. In so doing, they exaggerated the ignorance of the average person. This produced a spiritual pride that led them to believe that true understanding existed in their teachings.

Then Nicodemus, who had spoken with Jesus earlier (3:1–21), reminded them that no one was to be judged without a hearing. They responded with the firm conviction that no prophet could come from Galilee.

A SINLESS JUDGE (7:53–8:11)

The teachers of the Law and the Pharisees brought to Jesus a woman who had been caught in adultery. They wanted Him to pronounce proper judgment upon her. The Pharisees' purpose was to trap Jesus. If He neglected to suggest a stoning, as the Law required, He could be charged with being a lawbreaker. If, however, Jesus did advocate stoning, then He would bring the wrath of the Roman government upon Himself. How did Jesus handle this dilemma? "If any one of you is without sin, let him be the first to throw a stone at her" (v. 7).

Jesus didn't break the Law; yet, He ensured that the woman wouldn't be stoned. When everyone had left, Jesus addressed the woman's two greatest needs: self-esteem and a new life. For her self-esteem, He assured her that He, who was without sin, did not condemn her. For her deepest need, a new life, Jesus said, "Go now and leave your life of sin" (v. 11).

Over the years, this passage has been viewed differently, as some scholars have raised questions about its authenticity. Key reasons for this are that the text appears out of place and it differs from John's writing style. For the most part, however, Protestants and Roman Catholics alike regard this passage as authentic Scripture, even though it has been understood by textual scholars for centuries to be out of place.

This little story captures magnificently both the gracious, forgiving spirit of Jesus and His firm call to the transformation life (Gerald L. Borchert, *John 1–11* [New American Commentary], pp. 369–376).

■ *The story of the woman caught in adultery*
■ *captures both the gracious, forgiving spirit of*
■ *Jesus and His firm call to the transformation*
■ *life. Jesus addressed the woman's two great-*
■ *est needs: her self-esteem and a new life.*

QUESTIONS TO GUIDE YOUR STUDY

1. What authority did Jesus claim to have to back up His teaching?
2. What is the point of Jesus' teaching about the "streams of living water"? How did the crowd respond to this teaching?
3. Prior to His crucifixion, Jesus avoided attempts on His life. Why were His enemies repeatedly unsuccessful?
4. What was the purpose of the Pharisees' bringing the woman who had committed adultery to Jesus? What lessons can we gain from this event?

JOHN 8 -

Because John 7:53–8:11 is a unit of Scripture, 8:1–11 is included with the treatment of the preceding chapter.

THE LIGHT OF THE WORLD (8:12–30)

"I AM" Saying: The Light of the World (v. 12)

STATEMENT	SIGNIFICANCE
"I am the light of the world" (v. 12)	To know Jesus is to know God

Jesus' assertion that if people knew Him, they would know His Father is one of the most striking in all the New Testament. He was speaking to some of the most educated, most religious people who have ever lived. They were confident they knew God and understood His ways. But their rejection of Jesus shows they didn't know God. They knew only their own ideas about God.

Verses 12–18 constitute Jesus' fourth public discourse in John's Gospel. Here, the second of Jesus' "I am" statements occurs: "I am the light of the world" (v. 12). The relationship between Jesus and His Father is such that Jesus could say, "If you knew me, you would know my father also" (v. 19).

Teaching about His identity and nature, Jesus revealed that He was from above and not of this world (v. 23). Further, "if you do not believe that I am the one I claim to be, you will indeed die in your sins" (v. 24). This statement elicited a shocked, "Who are you?" (v. 25). Jesus answered that He was who He had always claimed to be—the one sent from the Father, the Son of Man.

■ *Jesus claims to be the "light of the world."*
■ *His relationship with the Father of is such a*
■ *nature that Jesus can say, "If you knew me,*
■ *you would know my father also" (v. 19).*

TRUTH THAT SETS ONE FREE (8:31–41)

Jesus emphasized that holding to His teachings is essential in order to claim to be one of His disciples. "If you hold to my teaching, you are really my disciples. Then you will know the truth, and the truth will set you free" (v. 31). Further, His teachings should be accepted as absolute truth. This truth, and no other, has the power to set a person free (v. 32). Many philosophies and ideologies claim to be based on truth, but all truth is God's truth. All claims to truth must be judged in light of God's revealed truth and knowledge. To adhere to a false view of reality is to be held captive by ignorance. The truth of Jesus sets persons free from all such bondage (v. 34).

Many have wondered how a loving God can condemn persons to hell. The proper response is that He does nothing of the sort. Individual persons condemn themselves by choosing to reject Jesus Christ and the truth He came to share with the world.

Notice that Jesus' promise that His disciples would know the truth and find deliverance in the truth is conditional. It hinges on the words "if . . . then." The condition is that disciples must "hold to" His teaching.

Truth is not assent to a proposition but trust in Jesus, who said, "I am the Way, the Truth, and the Life."

He is the one who liberates.

This "if . . . then" construction (v. 31) speaks of a condition and its consequences. The following chart reveals the structure of this passage.

The Pharisees refused to listen to the truth of Jesus, insisting instead on clinging to their own understandings. The idea of being free was too much for their pride: "We are Abraham's descendants and have never been slaves of anyone. How can you say that we shall be set free?"

Jesus' Promise of Truth and Freedom

CONDITION	CONSEQUENCES	PROMISED BENEFIT
"If you hold to my teaching"	1. You are My disciples	Discipline
	2. You will know the truth	Discernment
	3. The truth will set you free	Deliverance

Hold to

This is a characteristic word in John's Gospel. *Hold to* is a verb that means to "abide," "continue." Here it is used of holding to Jesus' teachings. Literally, "my teaching" is "my word." This is an active, not a passive, activity. To "hold to" the word means not only knowing the truth, but *living* it. "Continuance in the word (teaching) proves the sincerity or insincerity of the profession. It is the acid test" (A. T. Robertson, "The Fourth Gospel," *Word Pictures in the New Testament*, vol. 5, 149).

(v. 33). Perhaps the most telling verse is when Jesus stated that they had "no room" for His Word (v. 37).

■ *To those who continue in His Word, Jesus*
■ *promises knowledge of the truth and free-*
■ *dom from bondage to sin. The Jewish lead-*
■ *ers, however, found "no room" for Jesus'*
■ *teaching.*

WHO IS YOUR FATHER? (8:42–47)

If God was truly their Father, then they would love Him. Jesus made clear that His origin was divine, His mission was God planned, and His purpose was God willed.

People cannot hear what God has to say if they do not belong to God (v. 47). If people choose to listen to evil, then they close out the voice of God. The basic disposition of Satan is that of a liar, a perverter of truth, one who deceives everyone who allows him to direct their lives and thoughts.

THE ETERNAL "I AM" (8:48–59)

Desperate to discredit Jesus, the Jews accused Him of being a Samaritan as well as demon possessed (v. 48). Jesus denied the charge and immediately resumed His charge that they were living apart from God (v. 49). He added that if anyone kept His word, he would "never see death" (v. 51). The Jews were outraged. They saw Jesus as placing Himself above even Abraham. With one voice they asked in indignation, "Who do you think you are?" (v. 53).

Jesus replied that God glorified Him, that He knew God, and that He kept God's Word. Further, Abraham "rejoiced at the thought of seeing my day; he saw it and was glad" (v. 56). This brought utter amazement to the crowd. They challenged Him; for Jesus, a young man, was claiming to have seen Abraham.

Jesus gave one of the most important answers to any question posed to Him in the entire Gospel of John: "I tell you the truth, before Abraham was born, I am!"

Jesus then hid and slipped away from the Temple grounds. The timing of Jesus' death was not for the crowd to decide.

The only other time the phrase "I am" was used to describe someone was in Exod. 3:14, where God claimed that name for Himself. No identity statement could be clearer. Jesus claimed to be God Himself in human form. The Jews did not respond with words but picked up stones to kill Him for blasphemy. This is a "vivid picture of a mob ready to kill Jesus, already beginning to do so" (A. T. Robertson, "The Fourth Gospel, *Word Pictures in the New Testament*," vol. 5, 159).

- Jesus identified Himself with the eternal "I
- am," meaning that Jesus claimed an eternal
- existence with God. Reacting to Jesus' claim,
- the religious Jews sought to kill Him.

QUESTIONS TO GUIDE YOUR STUDY

1. In what sense is Jesus the "light of the world"? What truths does this statement convey?

2. Why are people who do not respond to the light condemned to hell?

3. Jesus said the condition for one's knowing the truth and being set free by it is "holding to" His teaching. What did He mean by this?

4. What were the implications of Jesus' claim to be the eternal "I AM"?

John continues his theme of *light*, which he introduced in 8:12. The sixth sign of Jesus' deity, the healing of the man born blind, occurs in this chapter.

SIN AND SICKNESS (9:1–12)

The Sixth Sign: Jesus' Healing of the Man Born Blind

MIRACLE PERFORMED	CHARACTERISTIC OF JESUS' POWER	RESULT OR RESPONSE TO THE SIGN
Jesus heals a man blind from birth	Master over *misfortune*	The Jewish leaders investigate the man's healing

Jesus saw a man who had been blind from birth. His disciples, reflecting a common belief of the day, wanted to know who had sinned and caused this man to be blind. Was it his parents or the man himself?

Refuting this entire system of thought, Jesus proclaimed that neither "this man nor his parents sinned" (v. 3). Instead, this man was there at that moment for God to work in His life in order to glorify Jesus.

Jesus spat on the ground, making a mud mixture of dirt and saliva, and placed the mud on the blind man's eyes. He then instructed the man to wash his eyes in the Pool of Siloam. The man did so and returned, seeing! The mud exercise was not medicinal but served as a means for the blind man to express his faith in Jesus'

Jesus performed more miracles related to giving sight to the blind than any other miracle. Such an activity was forecast in prophecy as a messianic act (Isa. 29:18; 35:5; 42:7). Jesus came to restore the sight of human beings who had become blinded to the things of God.

The rabbis taught that no one died unless there had been sin. Even a child could sin in the womb, they suggested, or even in the preexistent state prior to conception.

words. This sign pointed to Jesus as the giver of spiritual sight.

Jesus suggested a time would come when the work of the kingdom of God would not be able to continue. That time was not the end of His life, as the "we" in verse 4 suggests, but when the consummation of the age takes place. Until that day, God's people must do all they can to combat evil and do good in the name of Christ.

■ *Jesus' healing of the man blind from birth*
■ *was the sixth sign witnessing to His deity.*
■ *This sign pointed to Jesus as the giver of spir-*
■ *itual sight.*

THE POWER OF PERSONAL TESTIMONY (9:13–34)

The man who had been healed testified that he believed Jesus was a prophet (v. 17*b*). This was not the answer the Pharisees wanted to hear. Questioned again, the healed man said, "One thing I do know. I was blind but now I see!" (v. 25). This simple testimony has been the undeniable evidence for the Christian faith for centuries. His final words carry the greatest sting: "If this man were not from God, he could do nothing" (v. 33). The Pharisees became enraged, accused the man of being a sinner, and had him removed from their presence.

THE HEALED MAN'S CONFESSION (9:35–41)

After hearing that the man he had healed had been removed from the synagogue, Jesus looked him up. He offered one decisive question, "Do you believe in the Son of Man?" (v. 35). The

man responded, "Lord, I believe," and worshiped Jesus.

The healing of this blind man took place on two
levels: (1) at the physical level his sight was
restored; and (2) on the spiritual level he came
to faith in Christ. This man served as a model for
Jesus' entire ministry. The Pharisees who witnessed this event responded only in indignation
that Jesus would suggest they were blind (v. 40).
Jesus responded that if they were truly blind
they would be guiltless; but since they claimed
sight, their guilt remained (v. 41).

Now as then, some
people claim to see
but are spiritually
blind. And others
admit their blindness
and ask Christ to
restore their sight.

■ *Jesus' miracle of healing caused two different*
■ *responses. The healed man confessed his*
■ *faith in Jesus, while the Jewish leaders did*
■ *not believe and remained blind in their sin. It*
■ *is not possible to remain neutral before Jesus.*

QUESTIONS TO GUIDE YOUR STUDY

1. Why did the disciples and others assume
   the blind man's condition was the direct
   result of sin in the family?
2. What great lesson does Jesus' healing of
   this blind man teach us?
3. What was the effect of the healed man's
   testimony on the Jewish leaders? Why
   did they respond as they did?
4. What lessons can we apply from this passage of Scripture to our human condition
   today?

In chapter 10, John introduces the picture of the relationship between the sheep and their Shepherd. In covering this material, it might be helpful to keep in mind Old Testament passages that refer to rulers and leaders as shepherds: Ezek. 34; Isa. 56:9–12; Ps. 23.

JESUS IS THE "GATE" FOR HIS SHEEP (10:1–10)

"I AM" Saying: The Gate for the Sheep (v. 7)

STATEMENT	SIGNIFICANCE
"I am the gate for the sheep" (v. 7)	Jesus is the only entrance into the family of God

Jesus used this parable to explain His role as the gate to the kingdom of God. Shepherds regulated the coming and going of sheep between the sheep pen and the pasture. As the gate, Jesus decides who enters the family of God. It is He who gives salvation, security, and satisfaction to all who come into the family of God through faith in Him.

■ *Jesus characterized Himself as the gate*
■ *through which the sheep enter the sheep pen.*
■ *It is only through Jesus that one enters into*
■ *the family of God.*

JESUS IS THE "GOOD SHEPHERD" (10:11–21)

"I AM" Saying: The Good Shepherd (v. 11, 14)

STATEMENT	SIGNIFICANCE
"I am the good shepherd" (vv. 11, 14)	The Good Shepherd has personal concern for the sheep or persons in His flock

One of the great images of Jesus is as the "good shepherd" (v. 11). Jesus pointed to three dimensions of the shepherd-sheep relationship to communicate His relationship to believers.

1. He is the gate to the sheep pen, meaning that no one can enter the fold through any other means than Jesus Himself (vv. 1, 7–9). Only through Jesus Christ can anyone be made right with God and find eternal life.
2. Jesus leads His sheep. No other voice is the true voice of leadership (vv. 3b–5).
3. As the Good Shepherd, Jesus protects His flock—even to the point of death (v. 11).

Unlike someone who watches sheep for employment, Jesus is a Good Shepherd motivated by love for His sheep (vv. 12–13).

As the Good Shepherd, Jesus mentioned that there are other sheep who will listen to His voice and will one day be brought into the fold. More than likely, what He had in mind were the Gentiles who would come to believe in Christ. The idea is not that of many shepherds with many

Good Shepherd

John used an unusual term for *good.* It means "good, beautiful." It has the connotation of a winsome, attractive, and virtuous person. We might use this word in the sense of a model of perfection. Few portraits of Jesus have more appeal than His role of Shepherd. The "goodness" of this Shepherd abides in the fact that He does not spare Himself in looking after the sheep. The Good Shepherd willingly lays down His life for His sheep. This, in fact, is exactly what Jesus did.

flocks but of one Shepherd joining together one flock (v. 16; cp. Eph. 2:16). Jesus was not forced into being the Good Shepherd; He willingly took the role upon Himself, and for this He is loved by God (vv. 17–18).

■ *Jesus is the Good Shepherd. In this role, He*
■ *has personal concern for the individuals in*
■ *His flock. The sheep have His leadership and*
■ *protection. The Good Shepherd's love for His*
■ *sheep is so great that He would willingly lay*
■ *down His life to protect the sheep.*

DEDICATION, JESUS, AND HIS SHEEP (10:22–42)

The Relationship Between the Sheep and Their Shepherd (vv. 22–29)

These verses cover several key truths presented by John.

This section of chapter 10 takes place two or three months later at the Feast of Dedication. This feast celebrated the dedication and reopening of the Temple by Judas Maccabeus in December of 165 B.C., after it had been desecrated by the Syrian ruler Antiochus Epiphanes in 168 B.C. (cp. Dan. 11:31). This event is commonly referred to as "Hanukkah" or the Feast of Lights.

1. *The sheep hear the Shepherd's voice (v. 27).* Those who are Jesus' followers respond to His teaching.
2. *The sheep know the Shepherd (vv. 14, 27).* Jesus' followers have a relationship with Him and are completely committed to Him.
3. *The sheep follow the Shepherd (v. 27).* Followers of Jesus are persistent in obeying the teachings of Jesus and His Word.
4. *The sheep have eternal life (v. 28).* Jesus' followers are secure in the strong, protective hand of God.

Jesus also declared that "I and the Father are one" (v. 30). Jesus and God are not, according to the Christian doctrine of the Trinity, identical persons but separate persons who are of identical nature.

The Jews Attempt to Stone Jesus (vv. 30–42)

The Jews picked up stones to kill Jesus. They considered it blasphemous for a person to claim to be God (v. 33). Jesus responded to their anger by pointing back to the Old Testament where, in accord with the worldview of the ancient Near East, rulers and judges, as emissaries of the heavenly King, could be granted the honorary title "god" (Ps. 82). If they could accept that title for those to whom the Word of God came, how much more they should accept the idea that God's anointed should be called God (vv. 34–37). Jesus went on to say that if they did not believe His testimony, they could look at the works He did (vv. 37–39). However, this argument did not persuade His enemies, and they tried again to seize Jesus for execution.

■ *The relationship of the sheep to the Shepherd*
■ *is based on the sheep's belief in the Shepherd.*
■ *It is one of commitment and obedience on the*
■ *part of the sheep. The Good Shepherd loves*
■ *and protects His sheep.*

QUESTIONS TO GUIDE YOUR STUDY

1. What did Jesus mean by claiming to be the "gate for the sheep"?

2. Describe the relationship between the sheep and the Shepherd. What makes Jesus a "Good" Shepherd?

3. Describe the relationship between the sheep and the Shepherd. What key truths are associated with this relationship?

4. Why did the Jewish leaders want to stone Jesus? What resulted?

JOHN 11

The key event in this passage is Jesus' miracle of raising Lazarus from the dead. Although Lazarus's sisters, Mary and Martha, appear in the Synoptic Gospels (Matthew, Mark, and Luke), it is John who places so much emphasis on the raising of Lazarus from the dead.

LAZARUS DIES (11:1–16)

The sisters of Lazarus sent word to Jesus that Lazarus was very ill. Jesus assured them that Lazarus's condition would not result in death. Jesus delayed going to Lazarus for two days after receiving the message about his death.

His disciples urged Jesus not to go, for there were individuals who wanted to kill Him. Thomas, often called "the doubter," revealed the depth of his commitment to Jesus when he said to his fellow disciples: "Let us also go, that we may die with him" (v. 16).

JESUS' EMOTIONS (11:17–37)

One of the most moving scenes in the life of Jesus is at the tomb of Lazarus. Here we see not only the power of Jesus to raise the dead but also the emotions of Jesus moved by the grief of those around Him.

Martha's faith was evident as she approached Jesus, four days after the death of Lazarus, professing belief that He could have saved her dead brother. When Mary came as well and Jesus saw her grief and the grief of those with her, He was "deeply moved in spirit and troubled" (v. 33). Then Jesus wept (v. 35). He wept because of His deep love and affection for Lazarus and his sisters.

Lazarus

The name *Lazarus* means "one whom God helps." Lazarus was a personal friend of Jesus and the brother of Mary and Martha.

■ *Lazarus, whom Jesus loved, fell ill and died.*
■ *Jesus, moved by the grief around Him,*
■ *showed His human nature by weeping.*

JESUS: THE RESURRECTION AND THE LIFE (11:38–44)

The Seventh Sign: The Raising of Lazarus

MIRACLE PERFORMED	CHARACTERISTIC OF JESUS' POWER	RESULT OR RESPONSE TO THE SIGN
Jesus raises Lazarus from the dead	He is master of *death*	Many put their faith in Jesus

In a loud voice Jesus called out to Lazarus, "Lazarus, come out!" Still bound in his grave clothes, Lazarus came forth.

■ *Physical death may overtake the believer,*
■ *but spiritual death has no power over the*
■ *believer. A person who believes in Jesus*
■ *Christ personally shall continue to live.*
■ *Although death stands as the last and stron-*
■ *gest enemy, it is defeated through belief in*
■ *Jesus Christ. Jesus is both the Resurrection*
■ *and the Life.*

The Jewish people believed that the spirit of a dead person hovered over the body for three days before departing on the fourth day. The fourth day was when the process of decomposition began. Because of this, there would be no doubt for those who witnessed this miracle that Lazarus was dead.

THE SANHEDRIN REACTS (11:45–54)

The resurrection of Lazarus caused many people to place their faith in Jesus. It also led to a meeting of the Sanhedrin, the Jewish council.

The Sanhedrin was concerned about the growing influence of Jesus with the people. They acknowledged His miracles and feared that these would create such a following that even Rome would feel threatened. Rome might take away the authority of the Sanhedrin and do away with Israel as a nation.

Caiaphas, the high priest for that year, said it would be better if one man died than that the entire nation be removed. So, from that point on, Jesus and the Sanhedrin were on a collision course.

JESUS PREPARES FOR THE PASSOVER (11:55–57)

The religious authorities put out an order for people to report Jesus' presence so they might arrest Him. Jesus, aware of the Passover plot on His life, withdrew from Jerusalem to a wilderness area about twelve to fifteen miles away from the city. He stayed there with His disciples until the Passover season.

■ *Attending to their own interests and security*
■ *rather than the welfare of others and the*
■ *kingdom of God, the religious authorities*
■ *plotted to kill Jesus.*

QUESTIONS TO GUIDE YOUR STUDY

1. Jesus delayed coming to Lazarus while he was ill. What might have been His reason?
2. What significance does the sign of the raising of Lazarus hold?
3. Why did the Sanhedrin react so decisively toward Jesus' miracle of raising Lazarus?
4. Jesus avoided further confrontations with the religious leaders after learning of their plot to kill Him. What was His purpose in withdrawing?

What could testify more to the divine nature of Jesus than to exhibit the power needed to raise a person from the dead? Note that the raising of Lazarus serves as a foreshadowing of the power of God to resurrect all believers one day to fellowship and eternal life in Christ. Unlike Lazarus, who was raised only to die again, Christians will be raised to eternal life.

The Sanhedrin

The Sanhedrin was the high court of the Jews. In the New Testament period, it was comprised of three groups: the chief priests, the elders, and the teachers of the Law. Its membership reached seventy-one, including the high priest, who served as the presiding officer. Under Roman jurisdiction, the Sanhedrin was given great power, but it could not impose capital punishment (John 18:31).

JOHN 12

DEVOTION OR DEATH? (12:1–11)

This portion of John's Gospel contains a host of important elements, including Mary's devotion to Jesus, the deceit and corruption of Judas, and the judgment of Jesus on both Mary and the poor.

The Devotion of Mary (vv. 1–3)

The perfume Mary used to anoint Jesus' feet was very expensive, a luxury item for herself, selflessly given in devotion to Jesus. She poured it on the feet of Jesus in an act of humility; attending to the feet of another person was the work of a servant. Wiping the oil with her hair was also unusual, for respectable women did not unbraid their hair in public. Mary exhibited unrestrained love and devotion to Jesus that went beyond personal cost and concern for the opinion of others.

Judas's Deceit (vv. 4–6)

This is the sole passage in the Gospels that reveals the wicked character of Judas before his betrayal of Jesus. While John related Judas's dishonesty in hindsight, at the time Judas must have been highly esteemed by the Twelve because he was trusted with caring for the money bag.

Jesus' Judgment of Mary and the Poor (vv. 7–11)

Jesus affirmed Mary's act of devotion and linked it to His own burial. Mary did not intend for this to be the significance of her act, but Jesus interpreted it this way.

Jesus defended what Mary had done against the charge of the disciples that she should have sold

---

Mary of Bethany

Mary was the sister of Martha and Lazarus. All three were apparently part of an inner circle of Jesus' associates. John, in his Gospel, placed an emphasis on their status. Mary played a primary role in the episode of Lazarus's resurrection from the dead (John 11). In John 12, she anointed Jesus' feet with precious oil. This served as an important confessional function of anticipating His death. Given the sequence in John's Gospel, Mary is portrayed as a follower who was well acquainted with Jesus' ultimate destiny.

Individuals are often able to deceive others about their relationship to God, but never is God deceived, since He sees into the heart of every person.

Through the centuries, this statement of Jesus has been misinterpreted as an excuse to neglect the poor. The point Jesus made was that Mary's devotion at this particular time and place was worthy of the cost.

The palm branches which the crowd had were symbolic; they were used in celebrations of victory.

Hosanna!

Hosanna is a Hebrew or Aramaic word that is best translated as a prayer: "*save now*," or "*save.*" It was an expression of praise.

the perfume and given the money to the poor. "You will always have the poor among you" (v. 8), He declared.

- ■ *In a show of love and devotion for Jesus,*
- ■ *Mary of Bethany anointed Jesus' feet with a*
- ■ *very expensive oil. Because of His approach-*
- ■ *ing death, He linked this act to the prepara-*
- ■ *tion of His body for burial.*

PRAISING THE KING (12:12–19)

Jesus' triumphal entry into Jerusalem coincided with the Passover Feast.

The crowds responded to Jesus with shouts of "Hosanna!" and "Blessed is the King of Israel!" as He entered Jerusalem.

The Gospel of John emphasizes the royalty of Jesus. John's is the only Gospel that records that the people also shouted, "Blessed is the King of Israel!" (v. 13). The crowd's exultation, as well as Jesus' riding a colt, was not seen as the fulfillment of prophecy (v. 16) by the disciples until after His death, burial, and resurrection. This moment was perhaps the high mark of Jesus' popularity and influence. In only a matter of days, however, these "Hosannas!" would turn to "Crucify him!" (19:15).

- ■ *Jesus entered Jerusalem as the Passover*
- ■ *Feast was being celebrated. The crowd wel-*
- ■ *comed Him with shouts of "Hosanna!" How*
- ■ *the crowd's attitude would change in a few*
- ■ *short days!*

THE HOUR IS COME (12:20–36)

The request of some Greeks to interview Jesus brought a lengthy response from Jesus regarding the path before Him. Throughout the Gospel of John, Jesus had avoided situations that would hasten His death. But now the "hour" had come for "the Son of Man to be glorified" (v. 23). His death and subsequent resurrection is what Jesus had in mind with the term *glorified*.

At this point Jesus restated what He had said earlier—that death is a condition of life at its fullest.

Jesus understood that His death would bring life to many people (v. 24). Nevertheless, Jesus' heart was "troubled," which is all that John writes in relation to the Gethsemane passages of Jesus' final hours recorded in the other three Gospels. Jesus' troubled heart likely was the result of His bearing the weight of the sin of the world as a sinless being. This went beyond the physical and emotional agony that awaited Him. While He contemplated praying to God for deliverance, He remained on the course toward what God had willed for Him.

The cross would achieve salvation for those who believed, bring judgment upon the world for their refusal to believe, and defeat Satan's rebellion once for all. The lifting of Jesus on the cross would be the beacon that would draw all people—regardless of sex, race, social status, or nationality—to Himself for deliverance from sin (v. 32).

Verses 35–36 are the last words of Jesus' public ministry. They were a warning to the Jews to embrace salvation while there was still time.

Jesus often used observations from nature to illustrate spiritual realities (Mark 4:3–12). Earlier He compared the kingdom of God with a sower scattering seed. "Now He speaks of what happens to the seed that bears fruit. It must first die. It must lose its own identity, that the new plant may spring up" (Wm. E. Temple, *Readings in St. John's Gospel*, p. 195).

The Jews witnessed so many signs and other miraculous deeds of Jesus that it is difficult to understand why they refused to believe. The answer is found in prophecy. Quoting Isa. 53:1 and 6:10, John showed that the people were fulfilling what their own Scriptures had predicted (vv. 38–40). The Jews would not and could not believe.

Last day

There is a difference in meaning between the phrase *last day* (v. 48) and the much-used phrase "last days." The latter refers to the current period of time, begun when Christ entered the world (Acts 2:17; Heb. 1:2; 1 Pet. 1:20; Jude 18). The *last day* (singular), however, refers to the consummation of time and history when the great resurrection and judgment of all persons will occur (1 John 2:18).

■ *The time had come for the "Son of Man to be*
■ *glorified" (v. 23). His work of public minis-*
■ *try was finished. Jesus found the weight of*
■ *bearing all the sin of the world troubling, yet*
■ *He obeyed the will of the Father and stayed*
■ *His course.*

THE JEWS' REFUSAL TO BELIEVE JESUS (12:37–50)

They could not believe, not because their freedom of choice had been removed from them, but because they had purposely rejected God and chosen evil. Thus, God turned them over to their own choice.

In verses 44–50, Jesus summarized the theme of His teaching. This is likely a summary statement from the Gospel writer as Jesus closed His public ministry.

■ *In spite of all the signs they had witnessed, the*
■ *Jews refused to believe Jesus. Quoting Isa. 53:1*
■ *and 6:10, John showed that the people were*
■ *fulfilling what their own Scriptures had pre-*
■ *dicted. They had rejected God and chosen evil.*

QUESTIONS TO GUIDE YOUR STUDY

1. What prompted Mary to anoint Jesus' feet with oil? How did He interpret this act?

2. What does the term *hosanna* mean? Why was the crowd shouting this as they greeted Jesus? What were they expecting from Him?

3. As Jesus prayed in the Garden of Gethsemane, why was He "troubled"? What was His attitude toward the Father's will?
4. Isaiah predicted that the Jews would reject the Messiah. Why did the Jews reject Jesus and His teaching?

JOHN 13

Jesus was able to perform this act of utter humility because of His keen understanding of who He was, where He had come from, and where He was going (v. 3). This is a key to humility in all persons—a healthy and balanced understanding of who they are.

Foot washing in the Bible

Foot washing was an act necessary for comfort and cleanliness for any who had walked on dusty Palestinian roads in their sandals.

If Jesus, Lord and Teacher, washes our feet, how much more should we wash one another's feet (v. 14).

Jesus' public ministry has drawn to a close. Beginning with this chapter, Jesus emphasized His ministry to those who had responded to the gospel.

JESUS, THE HUMBLE SERVANT (13:1–17)

We see the love of Jesus for His disciples as well as those who would come to be His disciples in the washing of the disciples' feet. The servant motif, so prevalent in the Gospel of Mark (10:45), is revealed here as well. Servanthood is love at work (v. 1).

Jesus' washing of the disciples' feet had both an ethical and a symbolic sense. The ethical sense is emphasized in John 13:14–15, where Jesus presented Himself as the example of humble, loving service (cp. Luke 22:27). The command to do for one another what Christ had done for them was not to be confined to washing feet.

■ *We see the love of Jesus for His disciples in*
■ *His washing of their feet. The servant motif,*
■ *so prevalent in the Gospel of Mark (10:45),*
■ *is revealed here as well. Servanthood is an*
■ *expression of love.*

SATAN AND THE BETRAYER (13:18–30)

Betrayal is bad enough, but to do so after sharing a meal makes it even more heinous. At the moment Jesus identified Judas as His betrayer, Scripture tells us that "Satan entered into him"; and Jesus said, "What you are about to do, do quickly" (v. 27). This is the only use of the name *Satan* in John's Gospel, and it is unclear whether

Jesus meant possession by Satan or the motivation from Satan to evil. Judas's fellow disciples, however, did not realize what Jesus was referring to, thinking that it had something to do with Judas's responsibilities as keeper of the money bag (v. 28). Jesus had to be betrayed, but Judas did not have to be that betrayer. It has been said that the difference between Judas and Peter—one of whom betrayed Jesus and the other who denied Him—is that Peter sought forgiveness, but Judas did not.

"He who shared my bread has lifted up his heel against me" is a quotation of Ps. 41:9.

- *Jesus identified His betrayer, Judas Iscariot.*
- *Although Jesus was to be betrayed, Judas*
- *chose to be the betrayer. John tells us that*
- *Satan then entered into Judas.*

THE MARK OF DISCIPLESHIP (13:31–38)

After Judas's departure, Jesus made it clear that His time with the disciples was short (v. 33). The heart of this passage is found in verses 34–35: "A new command I give you: Love one another. As I have loved you, so you must love one another. By this all men will know that you are my disciples, if you love one another."

"There is a tradition that when John was an old man his pupils would set him in their midst, and he would say, 'Little children, love one another.' So the words which Jesus spoke in this tender scene stayed with him to the end of his life" (H. H. Hobbs, *An Exposition of the Gospel of John*, p. 216).

- *The mark of the Christian is the love which*
- *he or she exercises toward others. This love*
- *is not centered upon one's own interest, but*
- *rather upon the welfare of others. It is the*
- *kind of love that God extends to us.*

QUESTIONS TO GUIDE YOUR STUDY

1. What was the significance of Jesus' washing of the disciples' feet?
2. What were Judas's motivations for betraying Jesus?
3. The mark of a disciple of Jesus is love. What are the characteristics of love?
4. What makes Christian love unique?

The disciples had troubled hearts for several reasons: Jesus had informed them of His impending departure, He had revealed that a traitor was among them, and he had forecast that Peter would fail Him before all this was over. In this chapter, Jesus takes time to exhort the disciples and quiet their hearts.

THE REMEDY FOR ANXIETY (14:1–4)

Jesus urged His disciples to continue in their belief in Him and not let their hearts be troubled by what was to follow. Such words from Jesus regarding His upcoming departure cast a net of depression upon the meal. Then came the words of comfort from Jesus: "Do not let your hearts be troubled. Trust in God; trust also in me" (v. 1). Trust in God is the one true remedy for anxiety. Jesus completed the remedy for their concern by painting a beautiful portrait of the life that awaited them upon their reunion (vv. 2–4). The "many rooms" (v. 2) were "dwelling places" or "abiding places." These words indicated the permanency of the heavenly home of believers.

Heart

The *heart* is the center of the physical, mental, and spiritual life of humans. It is the "seat of spiritual life . . . the center of feeling and faith" (A. T. Robertson, "The Fourth Gospel," *Word Pictures in the New Testament*, vol. 5, 248).

- *Jesus' message in these verses is for His disci-*
- *ples to continue in their belief in Him so as*
- *not to let their hearts be troubled by what*
- *would follow—His death and departure.*

THE WAY, TRUTH, AND LIFE (14:5–14)

Jesus responded that a life given in belief and faith in Him would pave the way to eternal fellowship with Him (v. 6). Jesus' claim to be the way, the truth, and the life is of great importance. Jesus is not one of many ways to God, but *the* only way.

That Jesus embodies and proclaims the truth is a major theme throughout John's Gospel. Jesus also offers life itself, life through God the Father, the Creator and giver of all life.

"I AM" Saying:
The Way, the Truth, and Life (v. 6)

STATEMENT	SIGNIFICANCE
"I am the way and the truth and the life" (v. 6)	To the lost sinner who is ignorant and spiritually dead, Jesus is the Way, the Truth, and the Life

We need to remember that God is sovereign over all and subject to none. We are to pray in accordance with the will of God—as exhibited in the life and teaching of Jesus. When Christians pray in that manner, their prayers will surely be answered. To pray in Jesus' name is to pray in accord with His will and mission.

The last verse in this section has been widely debated as to its proper interpretation and application: "You may ask me for anything in my name, and I will do it" (v. 14). Was Jesus saying that we have unlimited power over God in determining what He will or will not do for us if we simply pray in Jesus' name? Clearly not, for this would be out of accord with the rest of the teaching of Scripture.

- *There is only one way to God, and this is*
- *through Jesus. To the lost sinner who is igno-*
- *rant and spiritually dead, Jesus is the Way,*
- *the Truth, and the Life.*

THE COUNSELOR (14:15–31)

John's Gospel pays much attention to the Holy Spirit. In fact, of the four Gospels, his Gospel has more to say about the activity of the Spirit. Here Jesus referred to the Holy Spirit as the "Counselor." Note that Jesus called the Spirit "another" Counselor, suggesting that the work of the Holy Spirit would take over Jesus' roles in the lives of the disciples.

Special Names for the Holy Spirit in John 14

NAME	MEANING
Counselor (v. 16)	He stands alongside, ministering to God's people
Spirit of truth (v. 17)	He communicates and testifies to God's truth through conviction

The role of the Holy Spirit as the one who "reminds" the disciples of what Jesus said and taught should not be overlooked as it relates: (1) to the writing of the New Testament and (2) to the ongoing life of the church. The church can expect this same ministry as it lives according to the teaching and encouragement of the Word of God.

The Holy Spirit is also the "Spirit of truth" (v. 17). The Spirit testifies to the truth of God in Christ and brings people toward that truth through conviction which leads to repentance and faith. Jesus' bottom line here is that the Spirit will continue to bring the presence of Christ into the lives of the disciples (vv. 16–18, 20).

Jesus also dealt in this passage with the relationship between love and obedience. To love Jesus is to obey Jesus (vv. 15, 23). If one does not obey Jesus, he doesn't love Him (v. 24).

Another Counselor

This term is translated from a Greek word (*paraclete*) that is a compound of two words: "called" and "to stand alongside." The term *Counselor* (*Advocate*, NRSV) is a legal term that goes beyond legal assistance to that of any aid given in time of need (1 John 2:1). Such a *paraclete* suggests an adviser, encourager, exhorter, comforter, and intercessor. The idea is that the Spirit will always stand alongside the people of God.

The Greek language has two words translated as "*another.*" One means "another who is different." The second means "another of the same kind." In this verse, the latter term is used.

■ *Jesus promised to send the disciples another*
■ *"Counselor" (the Holy Spirit) whose work*
■ *would take the place of His role in their lives.*
■ *As the "Spirit of Truth," this Counselor would*
■ *also communicate and testify to God's truth.*

QUESTIONS TO GUIDE YOUR STUDY

1. How is Jesus "the way and the truth and the life"? (v. 6).

2. What does Jesus' statement, "You may ask me for anything in my name, and I will do it" (v. 14) mean? How does this shape the prayers of believers?

3. Jesus told the disciples that He would send them the "Counselor" who was also the "Spirit of Truth." What do these titles mean?

4. When it comes to following Jesus, what is the relationship between love and obedience?

5. How does the Spirit's ministry of "reminding" believers apply to believers today?

Although John's Gospel does not have as many parables of Jesus as the other Gospels, John in this chapter records the parable of the vine and the branches.

THE TRUE VINE (15:1–17)

"I AM" Saying:
The True Vine (v. 1)

STATEMENT	SIGNIFICANCE
"I am the true vine" (v. 1)	To be a productive "branch," the believer must abide in Christ, the true vine

Here Jesus puts forth another of His "I am" statements. In this saying, Jesus asserted that He was the "true vine" and that God was the gardener (v. 1). With this symbolism, we can see two scenarios that are representative of the Christian life:

1. The one who is on the vine and producing fruit (Matt. 3:8; 7:16–20).
2. The one on the vine who is *not* producing fruit.

The productive vine was pruned for greater production, while the nonproductive vine was cut off for destruction. The key to producing fruits is one's relationship to the vine, to "remain in the vine" (vv. 4–5, 7). Apart from Christ, nothing can be accomplished (v. 5).

Branches that abide in the vine experience growth and, as a result, fruitfulness. Jesus

The Vine in the Old Testament

"The vine is one of the Old Testament figures used to illustrate the people of Israel. In Psalm 80: 8–19 Israel is the vine which God brought out of Egypt and planted in the ground which he has cleared to make room for it. The psalmist bewails the fact that it flourishes no longer, that its defenses are demolished and it is ravaged by marauders" (F.F. Bruce, *The Gospel of John,* p. 308).

suggested a threefold progression of spiritual productivity, as the following chart shows.

The Growth and Production of the Branches

Remain

This word means "to remain, stay, abide." Remaining in the vine is not a static or passive activity. In John 15:5, this word is in the present tense, which indicates continuous action. It is the branch that remains and continues to remain in the vine that produces fruit.

ACTION	RESULT
Abiding (v. 1)	Fruit (v. 2)
Pruning (v. 2)	More Fruit (v. 2)
Continued abiding (v. 5)	Much Fruit (v. 5)

Summary of the Parable of the Vine and Branches

Metaphor used: Branches growing on a vine

Lesson: The believer's need to abide in Christ

Jesus did not indicate the nature of the fruit, but Galatians 5:22 tells us that "the fruit of the Spirit is love, joy, peace, patience, kindness, goodness, faithfulness, gentleness and self-control."

Application: The main point is fellowship between the believer and Christ. To produce fruit, the believer must abide in Christ.

- *Jesus presented the parable of the vine and*
- *branches. The lesson of this teaching is the*
- *need of the branches (believers) to abide, or*
- *remain in, the vine (Jesus). Only by abiding*
- *in the true vine can the branches bear fruit.*

PLANTED IN CHRIST (15:18–16:4)

What is the result of a life that remains firmly planted in Christ? Jesus suggested that such a person would be hated by the world (v. 19). Christ Himself was hated and rejected because of the conviction that pierced the heart of every person whom He encountered. The Psalms predicted that Jesus would be hated without a cause (Ps. 35:19; 69:4). Because of the life and teaching of Christ, people know the truth and have no excuse for their choices that deny God's rule (v. 24).

This conviction will not end with the life and ministry of Jesus, for the Counselor, or Holy Spirit, will continue to testify to the hearts and minds of person about the truth and claims of Christ (v. 26)—as Jesus' disciples give verbal witness to Him (v. 27).

Why did Jesus share this with His disciples? He told them these truths so they "will not go astray" (16:1). Jesus prepared His disciples for the reality of the cross which they would also bear because of His name.

■ *Jesus was rejected and hated. The disciples*
■ *would also live in an atmosphere of persecu-*
■ *tion, hatred, and rejection following Jesus'*
■ *departure. Those who remain firmly in*
■ *Christ can expect the same kind of reception*
■ *which the world gave Jesus.*

QUESTIONS TO GUIDE YOUR STUDY

1. What are the two scenarios we can see in the parable of the vine and branches? What is the parable's main lesson?

2. How do the branches of the vine produce fruit?

3. What kind of fruit do Christians produce?

4. What kind of reception can the believer who remains in the vine expect from the world?

Because 16:1–4 is part of the discussion of the last section of chapter 15, those verses have been treated with that chapter.

THE WORK OF THE SPIRIT (16:5–16)

In Convicting the World (vv. 5–11)

The main line of defense the disciples would have in the coming period of persecution would be the power of the Spirit in their lives. In a carefully detailed statement, Jesus outlined the convicting work of the Holy Spirit, all related to the work and person of Christ.

1. The Spirit will convict the world in the area of sin that results from disbelief in Jesus (v. 9).
2. The Spirit will convict the world in the area of righteousness in light of the life of Jesus (v. 10).
3. The Spirit will convict the world in the area of judgment because Jesus defeated the prince of the world (Satan) who now stands condemned (v. 11).

The conviction of judgment is the result of God's judgment on Satan by the cross (v. 11). Although Satan had been "ruler" of the world, God showed Himself to be the true ruler of the world when He destroyed the power of Satan through Jesus' work on the cross.

Guiding the Believer (vv. 12–15)

Only through the Spirit can an individual be brought to repentance which leads to faith. It is not good works that elevate our status before God but the finished work of Christ on the cross. The Holy Spirit makes effective in the heart of the believer what Christ has done.

Convict

The word translated *convict* (v. 8) means "to expose, to convict, to cross-examine for the purpose of convicting or refuting an opponent, esp. used of legal proceedings" (F. Rienecker, C. Rogers, ed., *Linguistic Key to the Greek New Testament*, p. 254).

According to A. T. Robertson, this is "an old word for confuting, convicting by proof already in 3:29; 8:46" ("The Fourth Gospel," *Word Pictures in the New Testament*, vol. 5, 266).

The Spirit performs these ministries:

1. He guides believers "into all truth" (v. 13).
2. He glorifies Jesus (v. 15).

The Holy Spirit, the Spirit of truth, will guide disciples into all truth (v. 13). His purpose is to reveal Christ. The mark of the work of the Spirit, then, is whether Christ is made central and glorified in a believer's life.

■ *Jesus announced that He would send the*
■ *Counselor (the Holy Spirit) to be with the*
■ *disciples and to minister to their spiritual*
■ *needs. Jesus then discussed the convicting*
■ *work of the Holy Spirit, all related to the*
■ *work and person of Christ.*

"I HAVE OVERCOME THE WORLD" (16:17–33)

The disciples experienced understandable anxiety and confusion regarding all that Jesus shared with them. They were reluctant or unable to frame the question that was bothering them. But Jesus knew what they were thinking and spoke to their concerns (v. 19).

Jesus spoke straight with the disciples. He told them they were about to go through a time of deep grief while the world around them rejoiced—making their pain all the more intense.

Jesus didn't speak in abstractions. He told them that what they were about to go through was like a woman giving birth to a child. He promised them that on the other side of their grief, they would forget their pain—like the woman who embraces her newborn child. The joy they would experience on the other side of their grief would be something that no one could take from them.

Jesus told the disciples they would abandon Him, but He wouldn't be alone. His Father would be with Him.

His words of comfort were paramount with His passionate pleas to "Take heart! I have overcome the world" (v. 33).

I have overcome

The verb John used here means to "conquer," "overcome." The force of this verb indicates a continuing victory. Jesus' words, "I have overcome the world," were not so much a promise as a statement of fact. His victory also applies to us today. Through Him, we are also able to overcome the world. First John 5:1–5 teaches that those who believe in Him will be overcomers.

■ *Victory over the forces and circumstances*
■ *that invade our human lives are attainable*
■ *through Jesus, because He has overcome the*
■ *world by His work on the cross.*

QUESTIONS TO GUIDE YOUR STUDY

1. Why was it necessary for Jesus to send the Counselor? What would His role be?
2. Jesus described the convicting work of the coming Counselor. What is the nature of His work?
3. Why is the work of the Spirit so important in the life of a believer?
4. On what basis did Jesus declare that He had overcome the world? What does that mean to those who believe in Him?

Jesus ended His farewell discourse with a prayer—often called the "high priestly prayer."

INTRODUCTION TO JESUS' INTERCESSORY PRAYER

Jesus' Requests. His prayer included many requests on behalf of Himself, His disciples, and other believers (the church).

Jesus' Motives. Behind many of His specific requests we can often see His motive or purposes. Clearly, Jesus' motives were unselfish, as His dominant motive was that God would be glorified in the coming events of His death and Resurrection.

JESUS PRAYS FOR HIMSELF (17:1–5)

That

The Greek word *hina* translates into the English word *that* or the phrase "in order that." Sometimes *that* signals the content of what is being said. Usually, however, a clause that begins with the word *that* speaks of purpose. We can see that Jesus' prayer was full of purpose as the word *that* occurred nineteen times in His prayer.

Prayer for Himself Theme: Jesus' Finished Work of Salvation ("the time has come")

REQUEST	MOTIVE OR PURPOSE
1. Glorify your Son" (vv. 1, 5)	1. That God may be glorified
2. Restoration of Jesus' former status (v. 5)	2. That believers might have eternal life
	3. Jesus' earthly ministry was finished

Here we have the beginning of the longest recorded prayer of Jesus (17:1–26). In this first section of the prayer, Jesus noted that the cross would bring glory to Himself, for it was the will of God and the means of salvation for all who would believe.

■ *Jesus prayed for Himself. His requests were*
■ *that He would be glorfied and that He might*
■ *be restored to His former status. The key*
■ *theme of this section of His prayer was His*
■ *ministry: The work of salvation was finished.*

JESUS PRAYS FOR THE DISCIPLES (17:6–19)

Prayer for the Disciples
Theme: Sanctification
("sanctify them by your truth")

REQUEST	MOTIVE OR PURPOSE
1. Protection (v. 11)	1. That they be kept from sin and in fellowship with God
2. Unity (v. 11)	2. That they be united in purpose
3. Joy (v. 13)	3. That the joy of the Lord might be their strength
4. Sanctify them (v. 17)	4. That truth may liberate them from sin

Most of this section of Jesus' prayer was devoted to the welfare of the disciples. Jesus prayed specifically for their protection in the area of unity (v. 11), emphasizing again the importance of the unity of the body of Christ, the church. This is not organizational unity but interpersonal, relational unity. Jesus also prayed that they would be protected from the evil one, or Satan, who is more than active in the world and bitterly opposed to the things of God (1 John 5:19). Finally, Jesus prayed that God would sanctify the disciples through the word of truth (v. 17). Sanctification is the divine process whereby God molds us according to His holiness. It is bringing to bear upon our lives the moral absolutes of the living God in such a way that they affect how we live and think. Sanctification and revelation are directly related. Without God's revelatory word to our life, the process of sanctification cannot begin.

Sanctification

Sanctification is the process of being made holy, which results in a changed lifestyle for the believer. Christ's crucifixion makes possible the moving of the sinner from the profane to the holy so the believer can become a part of the temple where God dwells and is worshiped.

- *Jesus prayed for His disciples. The key theme*
- *of this section of His prayer was their sancti-*
- *fication.*

JESUS PRAYS FOR THE CHURCH (17:20–26)

Prayer for All Believers Theme: Glorification

REQUEST	MOTIVE OR PURPOSE
Unity (vv. 21, 22, 23)	That the Father's name might be known

Here Jesus' prayer turned specifically to those who would come to believe in Him through the disciples' message and testimony. He prayed for unity among His followers.

Father and Son are inseparably one—the Father in the Son and the Son in the Father. Jesus prayed that His followers will be in both the

"This display of unity is so compelling, so unworldly, that their witness as to who Jesus is becomes explainable only if Jesus truly is the revealer whom the Father has sent. Although the unity envisaged in this chapter is not institutional, this purpose clause at the end of v. 21 shows beyond possibility of doubt that the unity is meant to be observable. It is not achieved by hunting enthusiastically for the lowest common theological denominator, but by common adherence to the apostolic gospel, by love that is joyfully self-sacrificing, by undaunted commitment to the shared goals of the mission with which Jesus' followers have been charged, by self-conscious dependence on God himself of life and fruitfulness" (D. A. Carson, *The Gospel According to John*, p. 568).

Father and the Son in order to show to the world the oneness that comes from being rooted in God.

■ *Jesus prayed for all believers (the church).*
■ *The key theme of this section of His prayer*
■ *was the glorification of believers.*

QUESTIONS TO GUIDE YOUR STUDY

1. What makes this prayer of Jesus unique? What are its elements?
2. Sanctification is a very important concept in Jesus' prayer. What is the doctrine of sanctification? Why was it so important to Jesus in this prayer?
3. In this prayer, what do we learn about the relationship between the Son and the Father?
4. How did Jesus pray for Himself? for His disciples? for the church?

JOHN 18

In this chapter, the countdown to the cross quickens. The events leading up to Jesus' crucifixion begin: His arrest, Peter's denial, and His religious and civil trials.

JESUS' ARREST (18:1–14)

While in the Garden of Gethsemane, Jesus and the disciples were confronted by a band of soldiers, accompanied by Pharisees as well as Judas, Jesus' betrayer. We are not told the number of arresting officers and soldiers, but the usual size of a Roman cohort was six hundred men. This would not seem necessary for arresting one unarmed man and a handful of followers. Is it possible the authorities feared that Jesus had a secret army ready to spring to His defense or that others sympathetic to Jesus would come to His aid?

Jesus' concern for His disciples at the moment of His arrest is evident (v. 8). Peter's effort at defending Jesus was rebuked by Jesus. In spite of Peter's good intentions, the "cup" that was before Jesus had to be embraced.

■ *While in the Garden of Gethsemane with His*
■ *disciples, Jesus was approached by Judas and*
■ *a band of soldiers. They arrested Jesus to*
■ *bring Him before the high priests.*

The Synoptic Gospels (Matthew, Mark, and Luke) record that Judas betrayed Jesus with a kiss, the common gesture of greeting among friends. John's is the only Gospel that records that the attack on the servant of the chief priest was carried out by Simon Peter on a man named Malchus (v. 10). Luke records Jesus' healing of the man's wound (Luke 22:51).

Cup

The word *cup* is a metaphor for Jesus' suffering (Mark 10:38–39; Matt. 20:22–23). It is a metaphor here not for physical death in general but for the particular death which Jesus would suffer. In the Old Testament, the "cup" was often used for suffering (Ps. 75:8; Ezek. 23:31–34), as well as the wrath of God (Isa. 51:17, 22; Jer. 25:15; Rev. 14:10; 16:19).

JESUS BEFORE THE JEWISH AUTHORITIES (18:15–27)

Peter's First Denial (vv. 15–18)

The two interrogations may have been carried out by the religious authorities to give the sentence the semblance of a fair trial. Peter's first denial, all four Gospels report, came as the result of the challenge of a slave girl. She asked Peter if he was one of the disciples of Jesus, which Peter promptly denied (v. 17).

Jesus Before the High Priests (vv. 19–24)

Jesus was brought before Annas and Caiaphas. Annas was actually a former high priest, but he conducted the first interrogation before sending Jesus on to Caiaphas. The interrogations of Jesus by Annas and Caiaphas brought Jesus' response that He had taught publicly and that He had taught nothing in private that was not openly said to the crowds. This brought a blow to His face as if such a reply was improper when answering the high priest (v. 22). This blow was illegal in such questionings. Jesus' reply was the truth, and it should not have been rejected or reacted to with such violence. Note that John treated the Jewish trial with great brevity, devoting the majority of his narrative to the Roman trial.

Annas had served as high priest from A.D. 6 to 15. He still carried a lot of weight. Five of his sons served as priests; and the present high priest, Caiaphas, was his son-in-law.

The Drama of Betrayal (vv. 25–27)

Peter's second and third denials, followed by the prophesied crow of the rooster, are recorded just before the account of Jesus' interaction with Pilate (v. 38). John's narrative reveals two simultaneous plots:

- Peter's denials; and
- Jesus' interrogations and mock trial.

Both of those constitute a drama of betrayal: one by the people who should have received Christ as King and one by a person who should have remained loyal to Christ as King.

■ *The arresting soldiers brought Jesus before*
■ *Annas, the former high priest, and Caiaphas,*
■ *the acting high priest. His trial before the*
■ *religious leaders was illegal. During the*
■ *course of these proceedings, Peter denied His*
■ *Lord three times.*

JESUS' CIVIL TRIAL (18:28–40)

The Accusation to Pilate (vv. 28–32)

Next the Jewish leaders took Jesus to the palace of Pilate, the Roman governor. There is profound irony here. Their purpose was to have an innocent man put to death; yet they wanted to avoid becoming ceremonially unclean by going into the palace of the Roman governor.

Jesus' appearance before Annas and Caiaphas was anything but legal. John records several of the illegal aspects of Jesus' religious trial:

• It was held at night.

• Jesus was *assumed* guilty, and proven guilty.

• The court hired false witnesses to testify against Jesus.

• Jesus was mistreated while bound.

• The authorities did not allow Jesus a defense.

"I AM" Saying: The King (v. 37)

STATEMENT	SIGNIFICANCE
"I am a King" (v. 37)	Jesus' kingdom is a kingdom of truth

The Questioning by Pilate (vv. 33–38a)

Pilate's first question was perfunctory—almost a leading question in order to investigate the nature of the Jewish complaint. Jesus' answer was disarming, bringing a transparent reply from Pilate about the political tensions that had led Jesus to Pilate. Speaking in terms Pilate would understand, Jesus admitted being a King, but a King of far more than an earthly, temporal realm. Many people throughout Christian history have misinterpreted the kingdom of God in earthly terms.

As was His custom, Jesus then turned the discussion toward His mission. He informed Pilate that His kingly role was identified with testifying "to the truth. Everyone on the side of truth listens to me" (v. 37). Pilate's response was legendary: "What is truth?" (v. 38). Was it a serious question or a sarcastic response? We simply do not know.

Pilate's Offer of Release (vv. 38b–40)

Pilate went to the Jews and discussed their charges against Jesus. He announced that he found Jesus guilty of no crime. He decided to offer Jesus' release in celebration of the Passover. The Jews, however, demanded the release of Barabbas, a man who was an insurrectionist and a murderer (Luke 23:19). This was a twist that apparently Pilate did not anticipate. Honoring the crowd's choice, he sentenced Jesus to death.

■ *After questioning Jesus, Pilate was convinced*
■ *that Jesus had committed no crime. In an*
■ *attempt to free Jesus, Pilate offered to release*
■ *Jesus as part of the Passover celebration, but*
■ *the crowd insisted on the release of Barabbas*
■ *instead.*

QUESTIONS TO GUIDE YOUR STUDY

1. What did Jesus mean by "drinking the cup"?
2. Jesus' religious trial was plagued by many irregularities. What were these? Why did the high priests take the steps they did to have Jesus killed?
3. Pilate's question, "What is truth"? has been much debated. Was Pilate being sincere or sarcastic?

The Gospel of John records three major conversations between Jesus and persons who were confronted with the truth and the claims of the gospel. Nicodemus was a religious man who sought Jesus in order to pursue his spiritual questions (see John 3). The Samaritan woman was neither religious nor a skeptic but one who represented worldliness in its most common form. She was indifferent to the spiritual, living a life of moral self-indulgence (see John 4). Pilate, however, represents the modern secularist. Hardened to what would speak to his soul, he was neither open to nor inquisitive about the gospel.

Christ's suffering, death, and burial are the key events of this chapter.

THE SOURCE OF POWER (19:1–16*a*)

The physical and emotional torture Jesus suffered is beyond description. He was not only physically beaten but was also ridiculed and mocked. Perhaps as one last effort to have Jesus released, Pilate presented Him to the crowd after He was beaten to see if they could accept His liberation (v. 4). The Jews, however, insisted on His death because Jesus claimed to be the Son of God (v. 7).

Pilate's assertion that he had the power to free or crucify Jesus brought the following response from Jesus: "You would have no power over me if it were not given to you from above. Therefore the one who handed me over to you is guilty of a greater sin" (v. 11). While Pilate was not the initiator of the death of Jesus, he was not without sin in the matter.

- *In preparation for His crucifixion, Jesus was*
- *flogged, mocked, and ridiculed. In spite of*
- *His innocence, the Jews insisted on His death.*
- *Pilate complied.*

THE HOUR IS COME (19:16*b*–27)

Every word of John's Gospel leads to this moment, for the "hour" had finally come. In one last effort to cleanse Himself from guilt, Pilate had the title "Jesus of Nazareth, the King of the Jews" fastened to His cross. It was written in three languages: Latin, Aramaic, and Greek

Death by Crucifixion

Crucifixion was the method the Romans used to execute Christ. It was the most painful and degrading form of capital punishment in the ancient world. A person crucified in Jesus' day was first beaten with a whip consisting of thongs with imbedded pieces of metal. This scourging was designed to hasten death and lessen the terrible ordeal. After the beating, the victim carried the crossbeam to signify that life was over and to break his will to live. A tablet detailing the crime was often placed around the criminal's neck. At the site, the prisoner was tied (normal method) or nailed (if a quicker death was desired) to the crossbeam. The nails were driven through the wrist rather than the palm, since the smaller bones of the hand would not support the weight of the body.

(v. 19). To this point, every prophecy regarding the Messiah—even to the gambling for His clothes—was fulfilled (v. 24; cp. Ps. 22:18).

Present at Jesus' crucifixion were His mother, His mother's sister, Mary the wife of Clopas, and Mary Magdalene. Also present was the author of this Gospel, John, whom Jesus instructed to care for His mother (v. 27).

The Seven Sayings of Jesus on the Cross

SAYING	PASSAGE	EXPLANATION
1. "Father, forgive them, for they do not know what they are doing"	Luke 23:34	Jesus asked forgiveness for His enemies
2. "I tell you the truth, today, you will be with me in paradise"	Luke 23:43	Jesus offered paradise to the repentant thief on the cross
3. "Dear woman, here is your son" and "Here is your mother"	John 19:27	Jesus committed the care of Mary to His disciple John
4. "My God, my God, why have you forsaken me?"	Matt. 27:46	Jesus was aware of His alienation from God
5. "I am thirsty"	John 19:28	Jesus expressed agony because of the torture of crucifixion

The Seven Sayings of Jesus on the Cross

SAYING	PASSAGE	EXPLANATION
6. "It is finished"	John 19:30	A cry of victory, expressing that He had paid the debt of sin.
7. "Father, into your hands I commit my spirit"	Luke 23:46	An expressed confidence in the triumphant restoration of fellowship with the Father after death.

■ *Jesus was executed by crucifixion, the most*
■ *painful and degrading form of capital pun-*
■ *ishment in the ancient world. John, the*
■ *author of this Gospel, was present at the*
■ *Crucifixion.*

IT IS FINISHED: THE DEATH OF JESUS (19:28–37)

The actual death of Jesus was preceded with words fitting the narrative of John: "It is finished" (v. 30). What did Jesus mean by *finished*? The mission of Jesus, Son of God, was to die a substitutionary death for sinful persons. As a result of His death on our behalf, our sin was atoned, and eternal life through Jesus became attainable through a trusting faith.

With these final words, Jesus bowed His head and gave up "his spirit" (v. 30). This unusual way of describing a person's death suggests that

It is finished

This is one word (*tetelestai*) in the Greek text. It carries the idea of completion. The words *"It is finished"* mean that "the debt of our sin is all paid!" It is "a cry of victory in the hour of defeat" (A. T. Robertson, "The Fourth Gospel, *Word Pictures in the New Testament*," vol. 5, 304). Of particular significance is that the Greek perfect tense is used, which indicates a completed action that has continuing results. This word could also be translated, "It is accomplished."

The author of this Gospel, the apostle John, then offered his testimony that he was a witness to the Crucifixion and that even to the final moment every detail fulfilled the prophecies concerning the Messiah (vv. 35–37; cp. Exod. 12:46; Num. 9:12; Ps. 34:20; Zech. 12:10).

Jesus died voluntarily as an act of the will. After His death, a soldier pierced His side, "bringing a sudden flow of blood and water" (v. 34). From a medical standpoint, the mixture of blood and water from the spear's thrust was the result of piercing the sac that surrounds the heart (the pericardium) as well as the heart itself.

■ *When Jesus finished His substitutionary*
■ *work on the cross, He willingly and deliber-*
■ *ately gave up His life. With the words, "It is*
■ *finished," He gave up His spirit.*

THE BURIAL OF JESUS (19:38–42)

After the death of Jesus, most of the disciples were nowhere to be found. But two persons who had been afraid to declare their allegiance up to this point came forward boldly to care for the body of Christ. These two were Nicodemus (John 4) and Joseph of Arimathea, a rich member of the Sanhedrin who had agreed to the condemnation of Jesus (Matt. 27:57; Luke 23:50–51). Jesus was laid in a tomb following a traditional Jewish preparation.

QUESTIONS TO GUIDE YOUR STUDY

1. Why did the Jews insist on Jesus' death? In their view, what crime had He committed?

2. Read the account of Jesus' death and crucifixion in John 19. What physical suffering did Jesus endure? How do you think this suffering might compare to that of His bearing the weight of the world's sin?

3. What does the phrase *"it is finished"* convey?

4. What were the circumstances of Jesus' burial? Following Jesus' death, what was the apparent state of affairs among the disciples?

The Resurrection accounts differ in each of the Gospels, with each presenting its unique emphases of the event. In this chapter, John records three post-Resurrection appearances by Jesus, each of which has a dramatic effect on those whom He encountered.

THE RESURRECTION OF JESUS (20:1–18)

An Empty Tomb (vv. 1–10)

Mary Magdalene was the first person to arrive at the tomb of Jesus. Upon seeing the stone removed from the tomb, she ran to Peter and John, exclaiming that they had taken Jesus' body from the tomb. Peter and John ran to the tomb, finding only the strips of Jesus' burial clothes. Peter and John, as did Mary, failed to understand that the Resurrection had occurred (v. 9).

A Risen Lord! (vv. 10–18)

After all the others left the empty tomb, Mary stood alone weeping. Two angels appeared to her and asked her why she was expressing such grief. She said that someone had taken her Lord and she was trying to find Him. At that point Mary turned and saw Jesus.

The tenderness of the moment when He said, "Mary" and her recognition of Him and cry of "Rabbi!" (meaning "Teacher") is one of the emotional highlights of the entire Gospel of John. Jesus warned Mary not to "hold on" to Him, for He had "not yet returned to the Father" (v. 17).

"Robertson renders Jesus' prohibition as 'Cease clinging to me.' And since the verb form is a present tense this seem to be a good translation. She was not to continue clinging to Him, but was to bear His message to the apostles. This is suggestive to us. We are not simply to linger about the shrine of the resurrection, but are to go declaring the fact of it" (H. H. Hobbs, *An Exposition of the Gospel of John*, p. 283).

■ *Jesus had risen from the grave! His first*
■ *appearance was to Mary. His address to her,*
■ *"Mary," and her recognition of Him and cry*
■ *of "Rabbi!" is one of the emotional highlights*
■ *of John's Gospel.*

THE FORGIVENESS OF SINS (20:19–23)

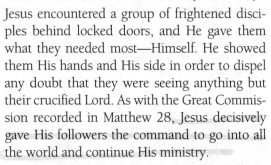

"What he commits to the disciples and to us is the power and privilege of giving assurance of the forgiveness of sins by God and correctly announcing the terms of forgiveness. There is no proof that he actually transferred to the apostles or their successors the power in and of themselves to forgive sin" (A. T. Robertson, "The Fourth Gospel," *Word Pictures in the New Testament*, vol. 5, 315).

God's forgiveness does not depend on human forgiveness, but rather forgiveness is extended by God as a result of individual response to the proclamation of the gospel by fellow human beings.

Jesus encountered a group of frightened disciples behind locked doors, and He gave them what they needed most—Himself. He showed them His hands and His side in order to dispel any doubt that they were seeing anything but their crucified Lord. As with the Great Commission recorded in Matthew 28, Jesus decisively gave His followers the command to go into all the world and continue His ministry.

He breathed on them (v. 22) and commanded them to receive the Holy Spirit—who would be poured out upon them in fullness fifty days later, during the festival of Pentecost.

Jesus stated that if the disciples forgave anyone, they were forgiven, and if they did not forgive others their sins, they would not be forgiven. At first glance this is a remarkable statement that seems out of step with the role and authority of the disciples. It was not the disciples who could forgive sins but Jesus. The literal reading from the Greek text is more clear, stating, "Those whose sins you forgive have already been forgiven; those whose sins you do not forgive have not been forgiven."

■ *John's second recorded post-Resurrection*
■ *appearance by Jesus was to His disciples. He*
■ *appeared to them behind their locked doors.*
■ *They rejoiced at seeing Him and received*
■ *peace and the spiritual power from Him to*
■ *complete their commission.*

THOMAS BELIEVES (20:24–30)

Thomas was not easily convinced of something that seemed impossible. Jesus directly addressed Thomas and instructed Him to place his fingers in the nailprints in His hands and the spear wound in His side. Then Jesus declared, "Stop doubting and believe." As long as Thomas doubted, he remained faithless and useless.

Whether Thomas actually placed his fingers in the nailprints and side wound, we do not know. It appears that all demands for proof were forgotten, as he responded, "My Lord and my God!"

Thomas's doubt was the same as that of many in the modern world. Unless he could see, taste, touch, and hear what was being presented as reality, he would not accept it as the truth. As Jesus noted, however, "Blessed are those who have not seen and yet have believed" (v. 29).

■ *Unless Thomas could see, taste, touch, and*
■ *hear what was being presented as reality, he*
■ *would not accept it as the truth. That he*
■ *demanded proof—and then believed—rein-*
■ *forces even more the credibility of the*
■ *accounts of Jesus' Resurrection.*

JOHN'S PURPOSE FOR WRITING HIS GOSPEL (20:31)

John's purpose statement is included here, following the Resurrection, in order that the reader might know the reason for this carefully detailed narrative of the life and teaching of Jesus. He desired that his readers:

You may believe

The force to the verb "believe" here is present tense. The idea John is trying to convey here is that those who believe *may keep on believing*. John's Gospel has had precisely that effect of continuous and successive confirmation of faith in Jesus Christ through the ages (A. T. Robertson, "The Fourth Gospel," *Word Pictures in the New Testament*, vol. 5, 317).

- Might come to believe that Jesus Christ is the Messiah; and
- That through believing they might have eternal life.

The purpose of the Gospel of John was to present Jesus as God in human form and that through faith in Jesus individuals would embrace salvation to eternal life.

QUESTIONS TO GUIDE YOUR STUDY

1. What caused Mary to recognize Jesus? What spiritual implications and lessons might we draw from this account of Mary's encounter with the Lord?

2. What were the results of Jesus' encounter with the disciples? Are there implications from the results of that encounter that apply to believers today?

3. How was Thomas typical of many nonbelievers today? What was the value of John's including the account about Thomas?

4. What was John's stated purpose for his Gospel?

- -

John's Gospel begins with a prologue and ends with an epilogue. A particular benefit of this epilogue is that we learn what happened between Simon Peter and Jesus and how Peter's denial of Jesus eventually concluded.

MIRACLES CONTINUE (21:1–14)

A Night of Failure (vv. 1–3)
Peter decided to return to his previous trade—fishing. He announced to the other disciples that he was going fishing, and six others joined him. Although nighttime was the usual time for fishing, the disciples fished all night without a catch.

A Morning of Success (vv. 4–14)
At daybreak, Jesus was watching from the shore of the lake. He shouted a question to them across the water, asking how they had fared during the night. At this point, they did not recognize Him. Jesus then instructed them to cast the net on the other side of the boat. Desperate to try anything, they did so and caught fish! Then one of the disciples recognized Jesus. Then they joined Him for breakfast.

The miraculous catch of fish and Jesus' fellowship with the disciples constitutes the third recorded appearance of Jesus following His resurrection. Here Jesus demonstrated again His power over the natural world.

153 fish

Some have found significance in the number of fish the disciples caught, citing the belief of the ancients that there were 153 kinds of fish. This would indicate that the gospel would include all persons and that the net of the kingdom of God would be strong enough to hold all without breaking. Clearly the gospel is for all, and the kingdom of God holds everyone.

Jesus restored Peter before his peers. None of those present could ever forget this expression of mercy and forgiveness. This was a defining moment in how the Lord deals with His own when they stumble and fall.

■ *Peter and six other disciples went fishing*
■ *throughout the night, but by morning they*
■ *had nothing to show for their work. Follow-*
■ *ing Jesus' instruction, they cast their nets on*
■ *the other side of the boat, catching 153 large*
■ *fish. Jesus used this experience to drive home*
■ *many lessons for the disciples.*

DO YOU LOVE ME? (21:15–25)

Following their breakfast on the shores of the Sea of Tiberias (Sea of Galilee), Jesus turned to Peter and asked him three times if he loved Jesus. By the third time, Peter was grieved that Jesus continued to ask him. He confessed that Jesus knew all things—that he knew Peter's heart.

"There is an early tradition that Peter suffered martyrdom by crucifixion. The first mention of such is by Tertullian who makes reference to John 21:18. Later Origen said he was crucified head downwards. This was said to be at Peter's own request, since, having denied his Lord, he did not deserve to die as He did with his head upwards" (H. H. Hobbs, *An Exposition of the Gospel of John*, p. 294).

It's no accident that Jesus asked Peter three times concerning his love. Peter had denied the Lord three times.

Following each affirmation of love, Jesus gave Peter a commission:

- "Tend My lambs."
- "Shepherd My sheep."
- "Tend My sheep."

Jesus then told the kind of death Peter would die to glorify God.

The final words of the Gospel of John change from firsthand narrative to a plural perspective. Not everything from the life of Christ was recorded, but only those things the author felt supported the goal of leading individuals to belief in Jesus as the Son of God, who came to take away the sins of the world.

The Gospel of John concludes with a verification of the testimony contained in it: "We know that his testimony is true. Jesus did many other things as well. If every one of them were written down, I suppose that even the whole world would not have room for the books that would be written" (vv. 24b–25).

■ *Peter's three denials of Jesus were answered*
■ *in three affirmations of love and service. He*
■ *declared his love and loyalty, and Jesus*
■ *accepted his confession and gave him a min-*
■ *istering responsibility. Peter was to shepherd*
■ *the sheep of Christ's fold.*

QUESTIONS TO GUIDE YOUR STUDY

1. What has been suggested as the significance of the miracle of the catch of 153 fish?
2. What was significant about Jesus' examination of Peter's love for Him? What was Jesus trying to accomplish with His interrogation of Peter?
3. Drawing from the closing verses of this chapter, what was the author's strategy for developing and presenting his account of the gospel? What unrecorded aspect of Jesus' life would you wish to learn about?
4. This final chapter serves as an epilogue to John's Gospel. What unique information do we learn from it?

The following list is a collection of the source works used for this volume. All are from Broadman & Holman's list of published reference resources. They accommodate the reader's need for more specific information and/or an expanded treatment of the Gospel of John. All of these works will greatly aid in the reader's study, teaching, and presentation of the message of John. The accompanying annotations can be helpful in guiding the reader to the proper resources.

RESOURCES:
Adams, J. McKee, rev. by Joseph A. Callaway, *Biblical Backgrounds*. This work provides valuable information on the physical and geographical settings of the New Testament. Its many color maps and other features add depth and understanding.

Blair, Joe, *Introducing the New Testament*, pp. 91–101. Designed as a core text for New Testament survey courses, this volume helps the reader understand the content and principles of the New Testament. Its features include maps and photos, outlines, and discussion questions.

Borchert, Gerald L., *John* (The New American Commentary), vol. 25A. A scholarly treatment of the text of John that provides emphases on the text itself, background, and theological considerations.

Cate, Robert L., *A History of the New Testament and Its Times*. An excellent and thorough survey of the birth and growth of the Christian faith in the first-century world.

Carter, James E., *John* (Layman's Bible Book Commentary), vol. 18. A popular-level treatment of John. This easy-to-use volume provides a relevant and practical perspective for the reader.

Holman Bible Dictionary. An exhaustive, alphabetically arranged resource of Bible-related subjects. An excellent tool of definitions and other information on the people, places, things, and events of the Bible.

Holman Bible Handbook, pp. 606–31. A comprehensive treatment that offers outlines, commentary on key themes and sections, and full-color photos, illustrations, charts, and maps. Provides an accent on the broader theological teachings of the Bible.

Holman Book of Biblical Charts, Maps, and Reconstructions, pp. 86, 99. A colorful, visual collection of charts, maps, and reconstructions. These well-designed tools are invaluable to the study of the Bible.

Lea, Thomas D., *The New Testament: Its Background and Message*, pp. 153–280. An excellent resource for background material—political, cultural, historical, and religious. Provides background information in both broad strokes on specific books, including the Gospels.

Robertson, A. T., *A Grammar of the Greek New Testament in the Light of Historical Research.* An exhaustive, scholarly work on the underlying language of the New Testament. Provides advanced insights into the grammatical, syntactical, and lexical aspects of the New Testament.

Robertson, A. T., *Word Pictures in the New Testament,* "The Fourth Gospel," vol. 5. This six-volume series provides insights into the language of the New Testament—Greek. Provides word studies as well as grammatical and background insights into the Gospel of John.

SHEPHERD'S NOTES

SHEPHERD'S NOTES

_____
_____
_____
_____
_____
_____
_____
_____
_____
_____
_____
_____
_____
_____
_____
_____
_____
_____
_____
_____
_____
_____
_____
_____

SHEPHERD'S NOTES